〈発見型〉コミュニケーション英文法

Discovery Learning in English Structure for Communication

Miura Takashi

三浦 孝

Kenkyusha

目次 contents

このテキストの特徴

　このテキストは、筆者が大学の一般教養英語授業用に半期 15 回分を作成し、それを 3 年間かけて実際に授業で使用しながら、何度も改良を加えて作り上げたものです。

　内容は、基本的には英語の文法力定着を目的としたテキストです。しかし、従来のこの種のテキストには無い、かなり新しい方式を取っています。

　まず第一は、何千何万何十万とある文法事項を、広く浅く全て羅列する従来の方式を改め、どうしても必要な少数の文法項目を重点的に選び、それ以外の項目を思い切って省いた点です。（「必要不可欠な文法事項」とは、それがないとコミュニケーションが成立しない、あるいは成立しないと思われる事項です。）そうすることで、学習者に学びの焦点を示し、「何もかも覚えなければ英語が使えない」という誤った不安から解放することを目指しています。

　第二に、「文の主部と述語動詞の発見力」と「語順訳による直読直解力」を、全編を通して繰り返しスパイラル的に高めています。これによって、複雑な英文をも大きな視野で捉えるようになり、構造がしっかりした英文を生成し、自然でスピーディーなリスニング・リーディングのコツが体得できます。

　第三に、使用する例文や読み物は全部、学習者にとって意味あるものになるように工夫しています。例文は、学習者の興味関心に合わせて、明日にでも実際のコミュニケーションに応用できる、脈絡のあるものにしました。更に、各単元に 1 つずつ配置した長文（語数 140〜880 語・平均 355 語）は、より良い英語コミュニケーションを行うために役立つ知識や情報を集めて書き下ろしたオリジナルです。

　第四に、このテキストでは、学習者自らが文法ルールを発見するプロセスを取り入れています。そしてその文法ルールの発見を、教室の仲間との協働学習で行えるよう作られています。90 分という長い授業時間をずっと教師の説明を聞いている授業ではなく、また練習問題を解いて答の解説を聞くだけの授業でもなく、学習者が仲間と相談しあって課題を解決しながら学ぶ授業を可能にしています。

　第五に、実際に教室でクラスメートと英語を使うことを通して英語コミュニケーション力を身につける方式を取っています。そのために、各ユニットには、英問英答の課題を配置し、さらにユニットごとにコミュニケーション活動が添えられています。その内容は、英語学習のための単なる字面のコミュニケーションではなく、現代を生きる若者が個性・喜び・願い・あこがれ・悩み・心配・主張を仲間とシェアし語り合える内容となっています。

　「英語は決して難しくない」、「英語で語り合うことは面白い」、そう実感できる授業づくりに、このテキストが役立つことを期待します。

2020 年 9 月 1 日　静岡大学名誉教授　三浦　孝

このテキストの構成

Part 1 英文の基本ルール

ルール

　各 Unit で学ぶ文法ルールの要点を学習します。このテキストでは、「これさえ解っていれば、あとは実際に使うことを通じて習得していける」という最重要文法ルールだけを厳選して学びます。言い換えれば、このテキストは英語の文法ルールを漏れなく解説したものではありません。あくまでも、コミュニケーションできる力を支えるための必要最低限の文法ルールに限って学びます。（「必要不可欠な文法事項」とは、それがないとコミュニケーションが成立しない、あるいは成立しないと思われる事項です。）

長　文

　その Unit の中心となる長文にざっと目を通します。ここでは、全部を理解する必要はありません。「大体何が書かれているか」を推測しながら、vocabulary hints を参考にして、とにかく最後までさっと読み通してみましょう。長文の前に置かれた「Vocabulary Hints」は、読解を支援するためのものですが、直訳直解の力を伸ばすため、可能なかぎり英英辞書的な説明をしています。理解できない単語や文の意味は、前後の文脈から推測しましょう。

内容理解

　その Unit の長文の中心となるメッセージが読み取れているかどうかを確かめる質問です。この質問を先に読んでから、長文を読むやり方もできます。これは特に、テキストの後半で、長文の語数が多くなってきた時にお勧めします。内容理解の後半に、長文の内容に関する英問英答練習を入れています。英語で内容関連質問をする力や、それに英語で答える力を徐々に養成するためです。

英問英答

　読んだ長文の内容について、英語の質問に英語で答える活動です。これは、読んだ長文の内容をより深く理解する力を養いながら、英語で質問する力、英語の質問に英文で答える力の養成に役立ちます。Unit 5 までは、答の英文を穴埋め式にして、答えやすくしてあります。これは、答の英文の組み立て方への慣れを作るためです。Unit 6 からは、答の英文を自力で作る方式になります。

発見学習

その課で学習した文法事項が、長文のどこに出現しているかを、探し出す活動です。文法が実際にどう働いているかを、文脈の中で確認します。目指すのは、言語データの中から自ら言語ルールを抽出できる力の養成です。ここは学習者の小グループで、お互いに知恵を出し合いながら、協力して課題に取り組みましょう。

語順訳

その Unit の長文の中の難しそうな文について、語順訳をして意味と文構造を確認します。（きちんと日本語らしい語順に訳したい人の場合は、必ずしも語順訳にこだわる必要ありません。）もしも、ここで扱っている以外で、難解な文があった時は、先生にそれを知らせてください。

練習

その Unit で学んだルールを実際に使って、自分の文を作ることを通して、理解を確認します。

Part 2 コミュニケーション活動集

その課で学習した内容に関連して、学習者の小グループで英語で話しあい、自分を表現し、お互いを理解する活動です。

自転車に乗るスキルと同じように、言語のルールはそれを理屈として知っていれば使えるというものではありません。実際に話したり書く必要に迫られて、思い出し・応用し・切り抜けることを通じて、体得されていくものです。ですから、言語を実際に意味ある場面で使う機会は、言語の習得に不可欠です。

今日、世界の英語話者の 70％以上は、非英語圏の人々ですから、日本人同士英語で話し合うことも、十分に効果が期待できます。特に、間を置かずに相づちを打ち、聞き返し、共感を表し、提案や賛同や質問ができるようにしましょう。

なお、クラスの状況によっては、このコミュニケーション活動を授業の最初に持って行くことも可能です。これは特に、英語で話し合うことに慣れているクラスにお勧めします。

以上のように、このテキストは参加型のアクティビティーやタスクを中心に編成されているため、「学生は授業で何をしたらよいか」が明確です。このため、オンライン授業で用いた場合にも、「タスクの提示→個人あるいはグループでのタスク活動→タスクの答の共有」のサイクルで授業が回ってゆき、受講者を退屈させることなく、適度な緊張感を持った授業が実現できます。なお🔊のマークは研究社のホームページからダウンロードできる朗読音声です。

英文の基本ルール

Unit 1A
主部と述語動詞

<small>S</small> <small>V</small>

ルール

---

1. 英文は、「〜は」を表す部分（主部）と、「〜だ/〜する」を表す部分（述部）でできています。

①

My friend Mei's dream 私の友人のメイの夢は	is to build a man-powered airplane that can fly for more than two hours. 2時間以上飛行できる人力飛行機を作ることです。
「〜は」を表す部分（主部）	「〜だ」を表す部分（述部）

②

The young woman with a dream その夢見る若い女性は	studies aeronautics at a technical college to realize her dream. その夢を実現するために工業大学で航空学を勉強します。
「〜は」を表す部分（主部）	「〜する」を表す部分（述部）

2. 本書では、**主部**を略して S と呼びます。

主部の中心となる**名詞**を「主語」と呼びます。

My friend Mei's **dream** ――――――→ 主語（S）

The young **woman** with a dream

主部（S）

3. **述部**の中心となる**動詞**を**述語動詞**と呼びます。本書では、**述語動詞**を略して V と呼びます。

述語動詞（V）

My friend Mei's dream	is to build a man-powered airplane that can fly for more than two hours.
The young woman with a dream	studies aeronautics at a technical college to realize her dream.

長文 : We Are 'More' Open

Vocabulary Hints: 次の 1〜9 の語の説明を、下の a〜i から選んで補いなさい。🔊

1. bomb	（名）	2. destroy	（動）	3. fortunately	（副）
4. injure	（動）	5. damage	（動）	6. customer	（名）
7. double-decker	（名）	8. sign	（名）	9. essence	（名）

説明

a. 看板	b. 爆弾	c. 損害を与える	d. 傷つける	e. 破壊する
f. 本質	g. luckily	h. a bus that has two floors		
i. someone who buys something from a shop				

内容理解 🔊

1．第二次世界大戦中、ロンドンを襲った恐怖とは、何でしたか？

2．ある朝、デパートの壁はどうなっていましたか？

3．なぜ、デパートの看板の「Open（営業中）」に、'More' が書き加えられていたのですか？

During World War II, London was attacked by German airplanes many times. They dropped many bombs on the city of London. The bombs destroyed buildings and killed many people. "Tomorrow, it will be my turn to be killed," the citizens of London thought.

One night, German airplanes attacked a new corner of London, and one of the bombs hit a department store. Fortunately, nobody was injured, but the store building was damaged.

The next morning, the neighbors and customers saw what the bomb had done. The entrance of the store was blown off, and there was a hole in the wall as big as a double-decker. But people were more surprised when they saw the familiar big sign 'OPEN' standing at the gate, and 'MORE' was added before the word 'OPEN'. Do you understand this humor? This story shows the essence of British humor.

発見学習

上のストーリー中の各文の、S（主部）を◯で囲み、V（述語動詞）に下線を引きなさい（最初の 4 行は例として記入してあります）。

Answer these questions in English.

（1）Which city did German airplanes attack during World War II? – They attacked
_____.

（2）What did German airplanes drop on the city of London? – They dropped
_____ _____.

（3）What hit the department store one night? – _____ _____ hit the
department store.

（4）Who was injured by the bombing? – Fortunately, _____ _____ injured.

（5）What was damaged by the bombing? – The _____ _____ was damaged.

（6）Was the store open the next morning? – _____, _____ _____.

（7）What did the big sign say? – It said '_____ _____.'

語順訳

　語順訳とは何か——英語の語順は日本語の語順とは大きく異なっています。そのため、英文を整った日本文に訳そうとすると、うしろから前へ逆向きに訳したり、あちこち飛びながら訳すことになり、大変に面倒です。

正式訳

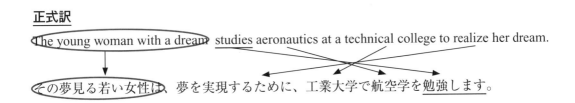

The young woman with a dream studies aeronautics at a technical college to realize her dream.

その夢見る若い女性は、夢を実現するために、工業大学で航空学を勉強します。

　それに対して、語順訳は英文を意味の塊りごとにスラッシュ (/) で区切り、塊りごとに前から後へと訳していくために、英語と日本語がすっきりと対応します。

語順訳

The young woman with a dream/ studies aeronautics/ at a technical college/ to realize her dream.

その夢見る若い女性は /　航空学を勉強する /　工業大学で /　自分の夢を実現するために

本書では、読書スピードを上げるために、語順訳[1]を使用することにします。

それでは、上の物語「We Are 'More' Open」を、スラッシュ (/) で区切って語順訳してみましょう。最初の4行は例として訳が記入してあります。

During World War II,/ London was attacked/ by German airplanes many times./
第二次世界大戦中に　　　/ ロンドンは攻撃された　/ ドイツの飛行機に何回も。　/

They dropped many bombs/ on the city of London./ The bombs destroyed buildings/
彼らは多くの爆弾を落とした　/ ロンドンの市街地に。　/ その爆弾は建物を破壊した　/

and killed many people./ "Tomorrow,/ it will be my turn/ to be killed,"/
そして多くの人々を殺した。/ 「明日は　/ 自分の番になるだろう　/ 殺される　」

the citizens of London thought.
ロンドンの市民たちは思った。

One night,/ German airplanes attacked/ a new corner of London,/ and one of the

bombs/ hit a department store./ Fortunately,/ nobody was injured,/ but the store

building was damaged.

1　語順訳の切り方のガイド
決まった切り方のルールはありませんが、大体は
　✔　カンマやコロン、セミコロン (,：;) の後で、
　✔　数語が集まってまとまった意味を表す語群の前や後で、
切ります。自分が簡潔に訳しやすいように切ればよいのです。本書では、よく用いられている切り方の例を、少しずつ紹介していきます。

The next morning,/ the neighbors and customers saw/ what the bomb had done./

The entrance of the store/ was blown off,/ and there was a hole in the wall/ as big as a

double-decker./ But people were more surprised/ when they saw/ the familiar big sign

'OPEN'/ standing at the gate,/ and 'MORE' was added/ before the word 'OPEN'./ Do

you understand this humor?/ This story shows/ the essence of British humor.

Unit 1B

be 動詞と一般動詞

ルール

英語の動詞は、「be 動詞」と「一般動詞」に分けられます。

1.「be 動詞」とは何か

① am, are, is, was, were, be, been をまとめて「be 動詞」と呼びます。

② 「be 動詞」は「○は△である」という意味の文を作ります。

am, are, is, was, were, be, been の使い分け方

主語が	時間が	肯定文で	否定文で	疑問文で
私	現在形	I **am** a student.	I **am not** a student. （I'm not）	**Am** I a student?
あなた		You **are** a student.	You **are not** a student. （aren't）	**Are** you a student?
彼 / 彼女 / それ		He/ She **is** a student.	He/She **is not** a student. （isn't）	**Is** he/she a student?
私たち		We **are** students.	We **are not** students.	**Are** we students?
あなた方		You **are** students.	You **are not** students.	**Are** you students?
彼ら / それら		They **are** students.	They **are not** students.	**Are** they students?
私	過去形	I **was** a student.	I **was not** a student. （wasn't）	**Was** I a student?
あなた		You **were** a student.	You **were not** a student. （weren't）	**Were** you a student?
彼 / 彼女 / それ		He/ She **was** a student.	He/She **was not** a student.	**Was** he/she a student?
私たち		We **were** students.	We **were not** students.	**Were** we students?
あなた方		You **were** students.	You **were not** students.	**Were** you students?
彼ら / それら		They **were** students.	They **were not** students.	**Were** they students?

＊ be（原形）と been（過去分詞形）の使われ方については、Unit 2A, 2B, 3, 5A, 7 でも学習します。

2.「一般動詞」とは何か

① 一般動詞は、数えられないくらい無数に存在します。「be 動詞」以外の動詞はすべて「一般動詞」です。

② 「○は△する」という意味の文を作ります。

③ 主語が単数（つまり1人/1つ）でしかも 'I' や 'You' 以外の時、一般動詞には '-s' か '-es' が付きます。これを3人称単数現在（略して3単現）の 's' と呼びます。

④ 否定文や疑問文を作るには、① do, does, did のいずれかを加え、②述語動詞を原形にします。

一般動詞の肯定文・否定文・疑問文の形

主語	時間	肯定文	否定文	疑問文
私	現在形	I **play** the clarinet.	I **do not play** the clarinet. (don't)	**Do** I **play** the clarinet?
あなた		You **play** the clarinet.	You **do not play** the clarinet. (don't)	**Do** you **play** the clarinet?
彼/彼女/それ		He/She **plays** the clarinet.	He / She **does not play** the (doesn't) clarinet.	**Does** he/she **play** the clarinet?
私たち		We **play** the clarinet.	We **do not play** the clarinet. (don't)	**Do** we **play** the clarinet?
あなた方		You **play** the clarinet.	You **do not play** the clarinet. (don't)	**Do** you **play** the clarinet?
彼ら		They **play** the clarinet.	They **do not play** the clarinet. (don't)	**Do** they **play** the clarinet?
私	過去形	I **played** the clarinet.	I **did not play** the clarinet. (didn't)	**Did** I **play** the clarinet?
あなた		You **played** the clarinet.	You **did not play** the clarinet. (didn't)	**Did** you **play** the clarinet?
彼/彼女/それ		He/She **played** the clarinet.	He / She **did not play** the (didn't) clarinet.	**Did** he/she **play** the clarinet?
私たち		We **played** the clarinet.	We **did not play** the clarinet. (didn't)	**Did** we **play** the clarinet?
あなた方		You **played** the clarinet.	You **did not play** the clarinet. (didn't)	**Did** you **play** the clarinet?
彼ら		They **played** the clarinet.	They **did not play** the (didn't) clarinet.	**Did** they **play** the clarinet?

＊動詞には、現在形、過去形、過去分詞形と原形があります。原形と過去分詞形の使われ方については、Unit 2A, 2B, 3, 5A, 7, 8, 14 でも学習します。

Vocabulary Hints: 次の 1〜9 の語の説明を、下の a〜i から選んで補いなさい。◀))

1. cargo	(名)	2. leak	(名)	3. uninhabited	(形)
4. tool	(名)	5. goat	(名)	6. shelter	(名)
7. enormously	(副)	8. miss	(動)	9. by chance	

説明

| a. 山羊 | b. 道具 | c. 漏れ | d. 〜が無くて淋しがる | e. 偶然に |
| f. greatly | g. carrying goods | h. place to protect yourself | | i. where nobody lives |

内容理解 ◀))

1. Alexander Selkirk は、なぜ無人島に置き去りにされたのですか？
2. Alexander は、食料をどうやって手に入れましたか？
3. Alexander が島で一番困ったのは、どんなことでしたか？
4. Alexander が、故郷に帰って一番困ったのは、どんなことでしたか？

Do you know the story of Robinson Crusoe, the world-famous English novel written in 1719? It was based on a real person. His name was Alexander Selkirk, a sailor on a cargo ship named Cinque Ports. While sailing, Alexander felt that the ship was not safe enough: it had a bad water leak. One day the ship stopped at a small uninhabited island. Alexander asked his captain to repair the ship, but the captain refused to do so. So, Alexander chose to stay on the island rather than sail on the dangerous ship. The captain agreed and left him on the island – a lonely island in the Pacific Ocean 670 kilometers from Chile.

Alexander had only a few tools and the Bible. He caught wild goats for meat and ate wild vegetables. So, food and shelter was not a serious problem for him. But he suffered enormously from loneliness.

Four years later, in 1709, an English ship came to the island by chance. Alexander was rescued by the ship and returned to his home in England. He found his life there too busy and even missed the loneliness of the old uninhabited island.

Answer these questions in English.

（1） Who was Robinson Crusoe? – He was the hero of a _____.

（2） What was Alexander Selkirk? – He was a _____.

（3） What was the name of his ship? – It was _____ _____.

（4） Why did Alexander think his ship was dangerous? – Because it had a _____ _____ _____.

（5） Why did Alexander choose to stay on the island? – Because he thought it was safer than his _____.

（6） Did anybody else live on the island? – _____, _____ _____.

（7） What was Alexander's biggest problem on the island? – It was _____.

（8） How long did he stay on the island? – He stayed there for _____ _____.

発見学習

（1） 例にならって、上記の物語の中の、述語動詞に be 動詞が使われている文を抜き出しなさい。（なお、各文の主部（S）は◯◯◯◯でマークしてあります。）

　　（例） (His name) was Alexander Selkirk,

（2） 例にならって、上記の物語の中の、述語動詞に一般動詞が使われている文を抜き出しなさい。

　　（例） Do (you) know the story of Robinson Crusoe?

〈解答欄〉

（1） be 動詞が使われている文
・
・
・
・

（2）　一般動詞が使われている文

- ・
- ・
- ・
- ・
- ・
- ・
- ・
- ・
- ・
- ・
- ・
- ・

語順訳

次の文を語順訳しなさい。

（1）　His name was Alexander Selkirk,/ a sailor on a cargo ship/ named Cinque Ports.

（2）　Alexander chose/ to stay on the island/ rather than sail/ on the dangerous ship.

（3）　He found/ his life there/ too busy and even missed/ the loneliness/ of the old

uninhabited island.

参考資料

　一般動詞の過去形・過去分詞形の作り方には 2 種類あります。どの動詞が、どちらの作り方をするかについては、英和辞典の巻末にある「不規則動詞活用表」で確認しましょう。

＜規則変化の過去形＞	＜不規則変化の過去形＞
-ed／-d を付けて過去形を作る	それ以外の過去形となる
（例）	（例）
（現在形）I want some water.	（現在形）I catch a taxi.
（過去形）I wanted some water.	（過去形）I caught a taxi.
（現在形）I plant a tree.	（現在形）I go home.
（過去形）I planted a tree.	（過去形）I went home.

肯定文・否定文・疑問文

ルール

肯定文とは、否定語（not, never など）が含まれていない文章です。

否定文とは、否定語（not, never など）が含まれている文章です。

疑問文とは、「～は --- ですか？」のように、物事について尋ねる文章です。

このユニットでは、英語の否定文と疑問文の作り方を復習します。

1．否定文

英語の否定文の作り方には、動詞の種類によって 2 種類があります。

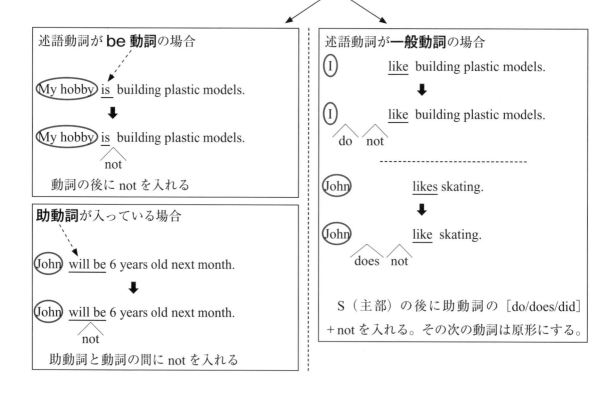

長文 : What Impressed Satomi the Most in Canada

次の文章は、聡美さんがカナダでホームステイした時の感想を述べたものです。

内容理解 🔊

1. 聡美さんがカナダで最も感激したことは何でしょう。
2. 聡美さんの質問への、クラスメートの答は何でしたか？

---

① Satomi is a college student in Japan. In the summer vacation, ② she took part in a one-month home-stay program in Canada. ③ She took classes in a college in Vancouver. ④ She stayed with her host family in Vancouver. During her stay, ⑤ she was very impressed with one thing. ⑥ In Canada, all her family members sit together and eat dinner every evening. She asked her Japanese classmates on the same program, "Do your Canadian family eat dinner together?"

Many of her Japanese classmates said "Yes". "I was very surprised!" they said. So, Satomi asked her host-mother, "Why do your family always eat dinner together?" Her host mother looked a little surprised and said, "This is natural. ⑦ We think our family is more important than our work."

練習-1

上の①〜⑦を、否定文に変えてみよう。

〈解答欄〉

①

②

③

④

⑤

⑥

⑦

2. Yes/No 疑問文の作り方

Yes か No かを問う疑問文の作り方は、動詞の種類によって 2 種類があります。

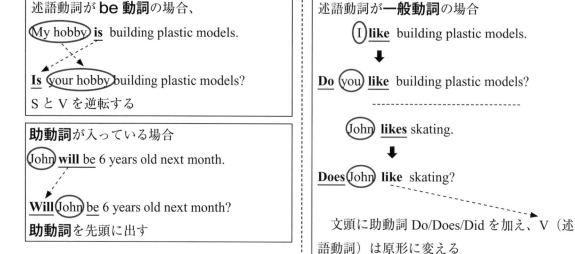

述語動詞が **be 動詞**の場合、

My hobby **is** building plastic models.

Is your hobby building plastic models?
S と V を逆転する

助動詞が入っている場合

John **will** be 6 years old next month.

Will John be 6 years old next month?
助動詞を先頭に出す

述語動詞が**一般動詞**の場合

I **like** building plastic models.
↓
Do you **like** building plastic models?

John **likes** skating.
↓
Does John **like** skating?

文頭に助動詞 Do/Does/Did を加え、V（述語動詞）は原形に変える

練習-2

上の①〜⑦の文を、Yes/No を問う疑問文に変えてみよう。

〈解答欄〉

①
②
③
④
⑤
⑥
⑦

3. WH 疑問文の作り方

Who, Whose, Which, What, When, Where, Why, How 等の疑問詞で始まる疑問文の作り方を学習しましょう。

慣れないうちは、Yes/No を問う疑問文を作って語順を固め、それから疑問詞を入れるという、2 段階方式がおすすめです。

（例）　　　Satomi studies aeronautics at a technical college. をもとに、波線部を問う疑問文を作るには、

①この文を、Yes/No を問う疑問文に変える。→

　　　Does Satomi study aeronautics at a technical college?

②波線部を疑問詞に代えて、文頭に出す。

　　What does Satomi study　　　　　　at a technical college?

（さとみは工業大学で何を勉強しますか？）

練習-3

次の各文の波線部を問う疑問文を作りなさい。

〈解答欄〉

（ア）Satomi is a college student. → （聡美の職業は何ですか？）

（イ）She took part in a one-month home-stay program in the summer vacation.
　　　→ （彼女は夏休みに何に加わりましたか？）

（ウ）She took classes in a college in Vancouver. → （彼女はどこで授業を受けましたか？）

（エ）During her stay, shc was impressed with the Canadian family life.
　　　→ （いつ、彼女はカナダの家族生活について感心しましたか？）

（オ）Her host mother looked a little surprised.
　　　→ （誰が、ちょっと驚いた顔をしたのですか？）*

（カ）All the family members eat dinner together because family is more important

---

* 文の S（主部）を疑問詞で問う場合には、語順は肯定文の語順となります。

than work.　→（なぜ、家族全員が一緒に夕食を食べるのですか？）

Unit 2B

未来表現

ルール

1. 英語には、「絶対にこの形で」という決まった未来形があるわけではありません。未来のことを表す形が4種類あります。

	例文	未来を表す形	ニュアンス
1	Linda **will give** an outdoor concert in Hibiya Park tomorrow.	will + 動詞原形	一般的な未来予想を表す
2	（ア）Linda **is going to give** an outdoor concert in Hibiya Park tomorrow. （イ）It **is going to rain** in the afternoon.	be going to + 動詞原形	（ア）「そういう予定で準備が進んでいる」を表す （イ）「この徴候で判断すると、こういうことが起きるだろう」という観測を表す
3	Linda **is giving** an outdoor concert in Hibiya Park tomorrow.	現在進行形を使った表現（Unit 6B）	確定度がやや低い予定を表す
4	Linda **gives** an outdoor concert in Hibiya Park tomorrow.	動詞の現在形	近い将来の、確定した予定を表す

2. このうち、最も一般的に使われるのは〈1. will + 動詞原形〉です。どの形にしたらよいか迷う場合には、この形を使えばよいでしょう。この 'will' は助動詞の仲間です。助動詞については、Unit 3 で詳しく学びます。

3. ただし、主語が「私」の場合、will には次のような注意が必要です。

（a）以前から決めた予定を表すには、〈be going to + 動詞〉を使う。

A: "Let's have dinner together this Saturday."

B: "Let's see. Unfortunately, I <u>am going to visit</u> my uncle in the hospital this Saturday. Maybe next time."

（今度の土曜日には、もう既に、おじさんをお見舞いに行く<u>ことになっているんだ</u>）

（b）今この場で決めたことは、〈will + 動詞原形〉で表す。

A: "I'm sorry to hear that. Listen, I am moving to Sapporo this Sunday. So Saturday is the last chance to have dinner with you. I will really miss you."

B: "Okay, then. I <u>will</u> <u>change</u> my schedule. I <u>will</u> <u>go</u> to meet my uncle on Sunday, and have dinner with you on Saturday.

（それならば、予定を変更<u>することにしよう</u>。おじさんのお見舞いは日曜日にして、土曜日は君と会食<u>することにしよう</u>）

    A: "That's very kind of you!"

4. "Will you---?" は、相手に用事を指示する表現です。

（例）Customer: <u>Will you</u> take me to Victoria Station?　客：ビクトリア駅まで<u>やってください</u>。

      Taxi driver: Certainly!　　　　　　　　　　　タクシー運転手：承知しました。

  この表現は、相手が当然するべき用事を相手に頼む時に使います。タクシーの運転手が、客の注文を聞くのは当然なので、この場合は適切な依頼表現です。

  一方、街頭で通行人を呼び止めて道を尋ねるような時には、相手が当然それに応える義務はないので、"Will you---?" で頼むのは不適切です。この場合は、"Could you" や "Can you" を使って、"Could you tell me the way to the station?" のようにお願いするとよいでしょう。

5. 未来のことであっても、「もし〜したら」「〜する時」「〜する前 / 後に」等を表す節（＝文中の文）では、現在形で表します。

                   ┌─────────────────────────┐
                   │ 未来のことだが will を入れない │
         ／└─────────────────────────┘

（例）"<u>If it rains tomorrow</u>, we will not go hiking." もし明日雨が降ったら、ハイキングは中止です。

                   ┌─────────────────────────┐
                   │ 未来のことだが will を入れない │
         ／└─────────────────────────┘

（例）"<u>When you arrive at the station</u>, please call me." あなたが駅へ着いたら、私に電話してください。

Unit 3

助動詞

助動詞には、will, can, must, may, shall 等々があり、話し手のさまざまな意向を表します。

→たとえば 'He runs a marathon tomorrow.' に助動詞を加えてみましょう。

He **will** run a marathon tomorrow.　　彼は明日マラソンを走るでしょう。（未来の予想）

He **can** run a marathon tomorrow.　　彼は明日マラソンを走ることができる。（可能性）

He **must** run a marathon tomorrow.　　彼は明日マラソンを走らなければならない。（それが唯一の選択肢）

He **may** run a marathon tomorrow.　　彼は明日マラソンを走るかもしれない。（不確実な可能性）

助動詞は V の直前に置かれる。

V は原形になる。

長文 : Do's and Don'ts When Speaking a Language
やるべきこと　やってはいけないこと

Vocabulary Hints: 次の 1〜7 の語の説明を、下の a〜g から選んで補いなさい。 🔊

1. ,that is,		2. honorific	（形）	3. superior	（名）
4. surname	（名）	5. add	（動）	6. boss	（名）
7. private	（形）				

説明

a. 上司	b. 加える	c. すなわち	d. 個人的な	e. last name
f. showing a sign of respect		g. a person who has a higher position		

内容理解 🔊

1．日本語では目上の人（例えば鈴木一郎氏）を呼ぶ時に、どのように呼ぶことが礼儀正しいとされていますか？

2．英語では、初対面の人（例えば Linda Brown 氏）を呼ぶ時に、どのように呼ぶことが礼儀正しいとされていますか？

3．英語で、お互いをファーストネームで呼び合うようになるきっかけは、何ですか？

Every language has its own way of addressing people. For example, in Japanese, you must use *sonkei-go*, that is, honorific language, when you speak to your superiors. Also, you cannot call your superiors by their first name; you must call them by their surname, adding '-san' after it.

Now, I will give you a quiz. Imagine you are working for a company and your boss is Ichiro Suzuki. What can you call him – 'Ichiro', 'Ichiro-san', 'Suzuki', or 'Suzuki-san'? The correct answer is 'Suzuki-san'. However, 'Ichiro-san' can be okay if you two are friends and having a private conversation.

How about in English? When you meet a person for the first time, it is safe to call the person by his or her surname, putting 'Mr.' or 'Miss' before it. For example, when you meet Linda Brown, you should call her 'Miss Brown'. Then, very often, the other person will say, "You can call me by my first name." or "Call me Linda." Then, you can call each other by your first names.

英問英答 🔊

Answer these questions in English.

(1) What does 'sonkei-go' mean in English? – It means _____ _____.

(2) When is the honorific language used in Japanese? – It is used when we speak to your _____.

(3) Do people usually call their boss by his/her first name in Japan? – _____, _____ _____.

(4) Imagine you are meeting a person named Mike Harvey for the first time. What will you call him – Mike, Harvey, or Mr. Harvey? – I will call him _____.

次の文を語順訳しなさい。

（1）　However,/ 'Ichiro-san' can be okay/ if you two are friends/ and having a private

conversation.

（2）　When you meet a person for the first time, / it is safe to call the person by his or

her surname, /putting 'Mr.' or 'Miss' before it.

（3）　Very often, /the other person will say,/ "You can call me by my first name." /or

"Call me Linda."

発見学習

上の文中の助動詞をマークし、その文の意味を考えなさい。（全部で 10 個あります。）

練習

個々の助動詞の使い方を学習しましょう。次の説明を読みながら、例文（1）～（7）の下線部に適当な助動詞と動詞を書き入れなさい。動詞は、be, hold, come, swim, use, cause, quit, carry, have, give のいずれかを用います。

（1）will　（過去形は would）

　①単純な未来の予想を表す。

　My mother _____ _____ 45 years old next month. （私の母は来月で 45 歳になるだろう）

　My family _____ _____ a birthday party for her.

（私の家族は彼女のために誕生会を開くだろう）（Unit 2B で既習）

② "Will you---?" は、相手に行動を指図するのに使われる。

_____ you _____ to my office right away?

（上役が部下に）（ただちに私のオフィスに<u>来てください</u>）

③ "I will---." には、「今この場で、私はこうすることに決めました」というニュアンスがあります。（Unit 2B で既習）

Bob: We are having a barbecue party next Sunday. Why don't you join us?

（僕たち今度の日曜日にバーベキューをやるんだ。一緒に来ない？）

Alex: Oh, I'm sorry but I'm going to take a medical check on that day.

（うわー、残念だな！その日は健康診断を受ける予定になってるんだ）

もしも "I will take a medical check---." と答えたら、「君とバーベキューするより健康診断を受けるのを選ぶことにする」というニュアンスを持つ。

(2) can（過去形は could）

① 「～する能力がある」を表します。

I _____ _____ 1,000 meters in breast stroke. （私は平泳ぎで 1,000 メートルは<u>泳げる</u>）

② 「～してよい」という許可を表します。

_____ I _____ your mobile phone?（あなたの携帯電話を<u>使っていいですか</u>？（カジュアルな場面で））

それに対する返事は、「はい、<u>いいです</u>」なら "Yes, you can." 「いいえ、<u>だめです</u>」なら "No, you cannot." となる

③ 「～する可能性がある」を表します。

Smoking _____ _____ cancer.（喫煙はガンを引き起こす<u>可能性がある</u>）

④疑問文や否定文の中で、「強い疑い」を表します。

"Our classmates, Shingo and Mami, are getting married. _____ it _____ true?" "No, it _____ _____ true."

「同級生の伸吾と真美が結婚するんだって。そんなこと<u>あり得るかな</u>？」「本当の<u>はずないよ</u>」

(3) must（過去形は無いので、had to で代用する）

①一般的に「〜しなければならない」を表す。ただし、"You must ..." の文では、「私はあなたに強制する」というニュアンスを持つ。

You ＿＿＿＿＿＿ ＿＿＿＿＿＿ our company.（社長が社員に）（君には会社を辞めて（quit）もらうよ）

＊客観的事情のためにその人が会社を辞めなければならない時には、"You <u>have to</u> quit our company." と表現する。

②「〜にちがいない」という強い確信を表す。

The rumor ＿＿＿＿＿＿ ＿＿＿＿＿＿ true.（そのうわさは本当に<u>ちがいない</u>）

③ "Must I submit my report by tomorrow?"（私は明日までにレポートを提出しなくてはいけませんか？）

→ "Yes, you <u>must</u> (submit your report by tomorrow)."（はい、<u>しなくてはいけません</u>）

→ "No, you <u>don't have to</u> (submit your report by tomorrow)."（いいえ、<u>しなくてもよろしい</u>）

〈注意〉"You <u>must not</u> (submit your report by tomorrow)." は、「あなたは明日までにレポートを提出<u>してはいけない</u>」（禁止）を表します。

(4) may（過去形は might）

①「〜してよい」という許可を表す。

＿＿＿＿＿＿ I ＿＿＿＿＿＿ your mobile phone?

（あなたの携帯電話を使っていいですか？（非常に丁寧））

それに対する返事は、

"Yes, you <u>may</u>."「はい、<u>いいです</u>」、"No, you <u>may not</u>."「いいえ、<u>だめです</u>」（軽い禁止）となる。

＊ただし普通の会話では、返事はもっと間接的に、"Sure, here it is."（はい、どうぞ）/ "Sorry, I don't let anyone use it."（すみません、人に貸すことができません）のように言う。

②「〜かもしれない」という推測を表す。

I have called him many times, but he doesn't answer. He ＿＿＿＿＿＿ ＿＿＿＿＿＿ angry.

（私が何度電話しても彼は出ない。彼は怒っているのかもしれない）

（5） shall（過去形は should）

"Shall I---?" の形で、「～しましょうか？」と申し出る表現。

"_____ I _____ your suitcase?"（あなたのスーツケースを運びましょうか？）

それに対する返事は「はい、お願いします」は "Yes, please."、「いいえ、けっこうです」は "No, thank you." となる。

（6） would

① will の過去形

② will とほぼ同じ意味を表すが、「もしできれば」というニュアンスを持つ。（「仮定法」という用法）

Would you come to my office?（Will you よりもやや丁寧になる。）

（7） should（＝ought to）

① shall の過去形

②「～すべきだ」（助言）、「～するはずだ」（確信）を表す

You _____ _____ up your seat to handicapped people on the train.
（電車の中では障害のある人に席をゆずるべきだ）

（8） 疑問文や否定文を作る do, does, did

これについては、Unit 2A で学びました。

注意

　助動詞は2つ並べて使うことができません。→必要な時には、片方を助動詞以外に言い換えて使います。

（例）　助動詞　助動詞

Jane will ~~can~~ drive at the end of the course.

（ジェーンは講習の終わりには運転できるようになるでしょう）

⇒ Jane will be able to drive at the end of the course.

　　助動詞　助動詞

You will ~~must~~ pass difficult examinations to become a lawyer.

（弁護士になるには、難しい試験に通らなければならないでしょう）

⇒ You will have to pass difficult examinations to become a lawyer.

Unit 4A

目的語（O）・補語（C）

ルール

---

1. SとVに加えて、目的語（略してO）と補語（略してC）も文の基本要素となります。
（注）OやCは、文中にある場合も、無い場合もあります。

2. 次の3つの文を比べてみましょう。

(a) My dog | is | a poodle.　　私の犬はプードル犬です。（my dog＝poodle）
　　(S)　　(V)　(C)

(b) My dog | eats | fish.　　　私の犬は魚を食べます。（my dog≠fish）
　　(S)　　(V)　(O)

(c) I | give | my dog | some fish | every morning.　私は私の犬に毎朝魚をあげます。
　(S)　(V)　(O)　　　(O)

(a) の文では、My dog＝a poodle という関係が成り立ちます。こういう関係の時、文法では 'a poodle' を 'My dog' の「補語」と呼びます。本書では、補語を略してCと呼びます。
V（述語動詞）がbe動詞なら、必ずS＋V＋Cの文になります。
補語になりうるのは名詞か名詞句・名詞節（Unit 4B, Unit 10）です。

(b) の文では、My dog＝fish の関係は成り立ちません。'fish' は 'My dog' の「食べる」という行為の対象になっています。こういう関係の時、文法では 'fish' を 'eat' という動詞の「目的語」と呼びます。このテキストでは、目的語を略してOと呼びます。
V（述語動詞）が一般動詞なら、一部の例外を除いて、S＋V＋Oの文になります。
目的語になりうるのは名詞か名詞句・名詞節（Unit 4B, Unit 10）です。
（補足）目的語を必要とする動詞を「他動詞」、必要としない動詞を「自動詞」と呼びます。

(c) の文では、give という動詞が、「my dog に」と「some fish を」の2つの目的語を伴っています。give の他に、tell / show / lend / bring / teach などの少数の動詞が、このように2つの目的語を伴います。

課題：次の文中の網掛け部分は O でしょうか C でしょうか、見分けましょう。

　　・O ならば波線を引いて、小さく（O）と記入する

　　・C ならば二重下線を引いて、小さく（C）と記入する

　最初の 3 文には答えが記入してあります。なお、主部（S）は丸で囲み、述語動詞（V）には下線が引いてあります。

答え方の例

(They) dropped <u>many bombs</u> on the city of London.
　　　　　　　　　　(O)

(The bombs) destroyed <u>buildings</u> and killed <u>many people</u>.
　　　　　　　　　　　　　(O)　　　　　　　　(O)

(The citizens of London) were <u>very afraid</u>.
　　　　　　　　　　　　　　　(C)

では答えを記入してみよう：

（Unit 1A で習った文）

① (German airplanes) attacked a new corner of London.

② (The neighbors and customers) saw what the bomb had done.

③ (They) saw the big sign 'OPEN' standing at the gate.

④ Do (you) understand this humor?

（Unit 1B で習った文）

① Do (you) know the story of Robinson Crusoe?

② (His name) was Alexander Selkirk.

③ (Alexander) felt that the ship was not safe enough.

④ (The ship) had a bad water leak.

⑤ (It) was a small island in the Pacific Ocean 670 kilometers from Chile.

⑥ (Alexander) had only a few tools and the Bible.

⑦ (He) caught wild goats for meat and ate wild vegetables.

⑧ But (loneliness) was a really serious problem.

⑨ (He) even missed the loneliness of the old uninhabited island.

（Unit 3 で習った文）

① (Every language) has its own way of addressing people.

② In Japanese, (you) must use *sonkei-go*.

③ (You) cannot call your superiors by their first name.

④ Now , ⃝I will give you a quiz.

⑤ ⃝You meet a person for the first time.

⑥ ⃝It is safe to call the person by his or her surname.

⑦ Imagine your boss is Ichiro Suzuki.

⑧ ⃝The correct answer is 'Suzuki-san'.

⑨ However, ⃝Ichiro-san can be okay if you two are friends and having a private conversation..

長文 : English Speakers in the World

Vocabulary Hints: 次の 1〜10 の語の説明を、下の a〜j から選んで補いなさい。 🔊

1. according to		2. native	（形）	3. in addition	
4. therefore	（副）	5. account for	（動）	6. ratio	（名）
7. non-native	（形）	8. exceed	（動）	9. total	（形）
10. billion	（名）				

説明

| a. おまけに | b. それゆえに | c. 〜によれば | d. 全体の | e. 〜を占める |
| f. 比率 | g. 1000 million | h. grow larger than | i. first-learned | j. not first-learned |

内容理解 🔊

1. 世界には、何らかの形で英語を使う人々がどれくらいいますか？

2. その中で、英語を母語としない人々の割合はどれくらいですか？

3. 今後、増加が予想されるのは、英語母語話者ですか、英語非母語話者ですか？

4. 日本の学生が将来の仕事や社会生活で英語を使う相手は、主としてどのような人々になるでしょうか？

The total population of the world is about 7.3 billion (7,300,000,000) people. How many of them speak English? According to *the English Club* (2019), about 1.5 billion people speak English all over the world. Of these speakers, about 380 million (380,000,000) are native English speakers in countries such as the U.S.A., U.K., Canada, Australia, New Zealand, South Africa, etc. In addition, about 1.12 billion (1,120,000,000)

Figure 1: The Ratio of English Speakers in the World

people use English as their second language or for international communication. Therefore, native English speakers account for only 25% of the total English speakers. (See Fig.1) In the near future, the ratio of non-native English speakers will increase steadily and exceed 80% of the total speakers.

In your future life, you will talk with a lot of people in English; in your study, on your job, and in your social life. More than 75 per cent of them will be non-native speakers, like you. Your success will partly depend on whether you can communicate well with those people.

出典：The English Club（2019）.「世界の英語人口 15 億」https://english-club.jp/blog/english-world-population/

英問英答 🔊

Answer these questions in English.

(1) How many people live in the whole world? –About _____ people live in the world.

(2) How many people speak English as their native language? – About _____ people do.

(3) How many people speak English as a second or foreign language? – About _____ people do.

(4) Is English spoken mainly as a native language in the world? – _____,

_____ _____.

(5) Is English spoken mainly as a second or a foreign language in the world? –
_____, _____ _____.

(6) What kind of English speakers will be the major speech partners for Japanese
people in the future? –They will be _____ speakers of English from other
countries.

発見学習

　上の長文で下線を引いた箇所は、文中で目的語になっていますか、それとも補語になっていますか？

語順訳

　次の文を語順訳しなさい。

(1) Of these speakers,/ about 380 million are native English speakers/ in countries

such as U.S.A., U.K., Canada, Australia, New Zealand, South Africa, etc.

(2) Therefore, /native English speakers/ account for only 25%/ of the total English

speakers./ (See Fig.1)

(3) Your success/ will partly depend on/ whether you can communicate well/ with

those people.

Unit 4B

「品詞」を意識しよう

　英語の単語は、下表のような品詞に分かれています。それぞれの品詞は、それぞれ異なる働きをしています。単語の意味を覚える時、品詞をも意識することで、その単語が更によく理解できます。

　辞書では、品詞は下表の略号のように表示されています。

品詞	略号	例	特徴
名詞	（名）	day, foreigner, Japan 等	文の主部（S）の中核やOやCとなる
代名詞	（代）	this, I, you, he, she 等	文の主部（S）の中核やOやCとなる
動詞	（動）	am, are, is, travel, work 等	主部（S）と結合して、S+VのVとなる
助動詞	（助動）	will, can, may, must 等	S+Vの、Vの前に位置して、意味を付け加える
形容詞	（形）	many, big, rural, easy 等	（ア）名詞を修飾（説明）する （イ）「〜は --- だ」の「---」（C）となる
冠詞	（冠）	a, an, the	名詞の前に付く
副詞	（副）	not, only, even, therefore 等	動詞・形容詞・副詞等を修飾（説明）する
前置詞	（前）	in, to, with, on, for, after 等	［前置詞＋名詞］で、句（まとまった意味の語群）を造る
接続詞	（接）	and, but, when, because, that 等	（ア）単語と単語を結びつける／（イ）文と文を結びつける

（注意）同じスペリングの単語でも、品詞が異なるものがあります。辞書を引くときは、その語の品詞が何であるかに注意しましょう。

　（例）I heard a strange <u>sound</u>.　私は不思議な音を聞いた。sound＝（名）「音」

　　　Your travel plan <u>sounds</u> interesting.　君の旅行計画は面白そうに聞こえる。

　　　　　　　　　　　　　　　　　　　　　　　　　sound＝（動）「聞こえる」

　　　You will have a <u>sound</u> sleep in this room.　この部屋なら君は深い眠りが得られる。

　　　　　　　　　　　　　　　　　　　　　　　　　sound＝（形）「深い」

長文 : Ice Breaking and Small Talk

Vocabulary Hints: 次の 1〜8 の語の説明を、下の a〜h から選んで補いなさい。🔊

1. rural	（形）	2. cafeteria	（名）	3. casual	（形）
4. offend	（動）	5. clinic	（名）	6. interactive	（形）
7. take turns		8. lubricant	（名）		

説明

a. 形式ばらない	b. 交互に〜する	c. 田舎の	d. 潤滑剤
e. 双方向的な	f. セルフサービス式の食堂	g. medical office	h. embarrass

(1)

内容理解-1 🔊

初めて会った人と気軽に会話を始める秘訣は何でしょう？

　　These days there are many <u>foreigners</u> in Japan, not only in <u>big</u> cities but also in rural areas. Some are traveling and others are working. Therefore, you have a lot of chances <u>to</u> start talking with them <u>on</u> the street, in a cafeteria, or on the train.

　　"Have you ever talked with foreign people?" I ask my students. <u>Most</u> of them say no. They say <u>that</u> they don't know how to <u>start</u> a conversation.

　　Starting a conversation is easy in English. First, smile <u>at</u> the other person. Second, make small talk.

　　'Small Talk' is a casual conversation. This is a <u>very</u> safe way of starting a conversation, and nobody <u>will</u> be offended by it. I <u>usually</u> start like this:

Example of a small talk in the school cafeteria

Honoka (Japanese)	Mike (Canadian)
Hi. Can I sit <u>here</u>?	
	Sure. Go ahead.
Thanks. <u>Do</u> you speak English?	
	Yes, I do.
Do you come here often?	
	Yes, <u>sometimes</u>. I love the food.
Me, too. I am a student from Japan. Are you a tourist, <u>or</u> do you work here?	
	I work here. I work at the clinic on the campus.
Really! By the way, I'm Honoka.	
	Hi, Honoka, I'm Mike.

(2)

内容理解-2 🔊

英語で、望ましい会話とは、どのような会話でしょうか？

Here is another hint for having a nice conversation: Make the conversation interactive, like playing tennis with your speech partner. Look at the conversation above. Both Honoka and Mike take turns speaking and listening to each other. That shows good manners in an English conversation.

(3)

内容理解-3 🔊

スモールトークは、何のために行われますか？

English-speaking people love to exchange small talk with new people. Small talk is a casual conversation on unimportant topics. Small talk is a good social lubricant. It helps people to relax with each other. Popular and safe topics for small talks are as follows:

話題（topics）	例（examples）
Weather（お天気）	"It's a beautiful day." / "It's freezing cold."
Home country（出身地）	"Where are you from?" / "Are you from America?"
Food（食べ物）	"How do you like the food here?"/ "Do you like Japanese food?"
Fun/ holiday plans（楽しみ / 遊びの計画）	"Are you having a good time in Japan?"/ " Which places do you like in Japan?"
Popular sports events（人気のあるスポーツ試合）	"Did you watch the football games last night?" – "Yeah, it was so exciting."
Complimenting（相手のちょっとした点を褒める）	"That's a nice tie."/ "I like your jacket. It looks good on you." / "Your bike is great." /"You speak Japanese well."

　日本人に対する外国人の苦情の中に、「外国人と見れば英語を話すものと決めつけてくる人がいる」という声が多くあります。Honoka が最初に "Do you speak English?" と確かめていることは国際的なマナーです。

発見学習

　上の文中に使われている下線の語の品詞は何でしょう。（注意：1つの単語が、文中の前後関係に応じて、異なる品詞として働くことがあります。どの品詞として働いているかは、文脈で判断しましょう）

1. foreigners		2. big	
3. to		4. on	
5. most		6. that	
7. start		8. at	
9. very		10. will	
11. usually		12. here	
13. do		14. sometimes	
15. or			

語順訳

　次の文を語順訳しなさい。

（1）　They say /that they don't know/ how to start a conversation.

（2）　Make the conversation interactive,/ like playing tennis/ with your speech partner.

（3） Both Honoka and Mike take turns/ speaking and listening to each other.

（4） Small talk is a good social luburicant. It helps people / to relax with each other.

英問英答 🔊

Answer these questions in English.

（1） What is a good way to start talking with new people in a relaxed manner? – It is to have ＿＿＿＿＿ ＿＿＿＿＿.

（2） What topics do people usually choose for a small talk? – They usually choose ＿＿＿＿＿ topics such as weather, food and sports.

（3） How can we make our conversation ＿＿＿＿＿? – We make sure that each of us has equal time to speak and listen to each other, like playing tennis.

Unit 5A

過去形と現在完了形

ルール 1

1. 過去形の形については、Unit 1B で既に学びました。

　過去形は、過去の事実を述べることだけに関心があり、現在どうなっているかには関心を持ちません。

　一方、現在完了形は、過去の出来事が<u>今にどう影響しているか</u>に関心があります。

過去形と現在完了形の違い	
1．過去形 形：S＋動詞の過去形 例文：Mike married Naomi. 意味：「そういう過去の事実がある」 （現在どうなっているかには関心が無い）	**2．現在完了形** 形：S＋have/has＋動詞の過去分詞形 例文：Mike has married Naomi. 意味：「だから今、マイクと直美は夫婦だ」

2. 現在完了形は、V（述語動詞）が［have（has）＋動詞の過去分詞］の形をしています。

現在完了形の作り方

形は：S（主部）＋ $\left(\begin{array}{c} \text{have} \\ \text{has} \end{array}\right)$ ＋動詞の過去分詞

意味：'have' の根本的意味と共通

I	have	climbed Mt.Fuji.
私は	持っている	富士山に登った経験を

3. 過去分詞とは何か？

　英語では、1つの動詞が何種類かの形に変化します。

　be 動詞は、次のように変化します。

原形	現在形	過去形	過去分詞形
be	am	was	been
	are	were	
	is	was	

一方、一般動詞は、次のように2つのタイプに変化します。

規則変化動詞				不規則変化動詞			
原形	現在形	過去形	過去分詞形	原形	現在形	過去形	過去分詞形
現在形と同じ	invent	invented	invented	現在形と同じ	eat	ate	eaten
	like	liked	liked		lose	lost	lost
	drop	dropped	dropped		go	went	gone
	marry	married	married		catch	caught	caught

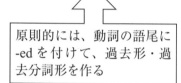

原則的には、動詞の語尾に-ed を付けて、過去形・過去分詞形を作る

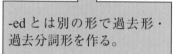

-edとは別の形で過去形・過去分詞形を作る。

4. 過去分詞は何に使われるか？

過去分詞は下表の (a) (b) のように完了形に使われるか、(c) (d) のように「～される」意味に使われます。

	例文	訳
(a) 現在完了形に	Mike has broken the radio.	マイクはラジオを壊してしまった。
(b) 過去完了形に（Unit 14 で学習）	Mike had broken the radio before I stopped him.	私が止める前に、マイクはラジオを壊してしまっていた。
(c) 受動態に（Unit 7 で学習）	The radio was broken by Mike.	そのラジオはマイクに壊された。
(d) 過去分詞の形容詞的用法に（Unit 7 で学習）	The radio broken by Mike was expensive.	マイクに壊されたラジオは高価な物だった。

長文：Junya's Part-time Job

内容理解 🔊

1. 淳也君と Texas BBQ House とは、長いつきあいがあります。どのようなつきあいでしょうか？

2. 淳也君は英語をどうやって話せるようにしましたか？

3. ある日、店のお客さんは、どういうことで困っていましたか？

淳也君（19歳）は、Texas BBQ House のアルバイト求人に応募しました。今、店長 Barbara さんから、採用面接を受けています。

B: Have you worked at a barbecue restaurant before, Junya?

J: No, I haven't. But I have eaten at your restaurant many times.

B: Really! I'm glad to hear that. We have run this restaurant for ten years, since 2010.

J: I know. I always enjoy your food.

面接の結果、淳也君は採用になりました。勤務初日、店長 Barbara は淳也をシェフの David に紹介します。

B: David, this is our new staff member, Junya.

D: Hi, Junya.

J: Nice to meet you, David.

D: Nice to meet you. You speak good English.

J: Thank you! I have been studying English for six and a half years. I have some English-speaking friends in Japan.

D: Very well. Okay, let's start cooking. Have you washed your hands yet?

J: Yes, I've already washed them very carefully.

D: That's fine!

ある日、淳也君は接客中に、大変困った表情のお客さん（C さん）を見かけました。

J: Is anything wrong?

C: Yes, it seems I have lost my wallet somewhere. I have no money with me.

J: Oh, really!

C: I'm sorry I cannot pay for the food now.

J: Okay, could you tell the manager? She'll take care of things.

Answer these questions in English.

(1) Has Junya got a job at Texas Barbecue House? — ＿＿＿＿, ＿＿＿ ＿＿＿＿＿.

(2) Who is the manager of the Texas Barbecue House? — ＿＿＿＿＿＿ is.

(3) How long has Texas Barbecue House been open? — It has been open for ＿＿＿＿ ＿＿＿＿.

(4) Has Junya visited the Barbecue House before? — ＿＿＿, ＿＿＿ ＿＿＿＿.

(5) Why can't the customer pay for the lunch? — Because she ＿＿＿ ＿＿＿＿ her wallet.

発見学習-1

上のストーリーを読み、現在完了形の V（have（has）＋動詞の過去分詞）に下線を引き、その文を和訳しなさい。

最初の 2 文には答えが記入してあります。

ルール 2

現在完了形は、過去のことを扱いながらも、「だから今どうなっているか」を伝えたいのです。これが、過去形との違いです。

現在完了形の意味	例文	現在完了形の意味	現在完了形が伝えたい意図
完了	Have you washed your hands yet? Yes, I've already washed them very carefully.	もう〜してしまいました	だから今、もう済んでいます
経験	Have you worked at a barbecue restaurant before, Junya? I have eaten at your restaurant many times.	〜したことがあります	だから今、〜について知っています
継続	We have run this restaurant for ten years. I have been studying English for six and a half years.	今までずっと〜してきました	だから今も〜を続けています
結果	I have lost my wallet somewhere.	〜してしまいました	だから今、こういう状態になっています

＊ 'have' には①現在完了形を作る助動詞と、②「〜を持っている」という意味の一般動詞、の 2 種類があります。混同しないようにしましょう。

Monta 君（28 歳）は 13 年ぶりに中学校の同窓会に出席しました。（Monta had a broken heart six months ago, and has had no girlfriend since then.）同窓会で、昔からずっと好意を寄せていたクラスメートの Honoka を見かけます !!　ぐんと大人びて、魅力的になった Honoka に Monta は勇気を振り絞って声をかけます。

M: Good to see you, Honoka. How have you been?

ここからは、Honoka の返事の形によって、展開が変わってきます。

課題　次のうち、Honoka が今独身である可能性があるのはどちらでしょうか？

H: You remember Ayataro, one of our classmates. I have been married to him for five years.	H: You remember Ayataro, one of our classmates. I married him five years ago.

修飾語を見分けよう

ルール

1. 英文の基本要素はS、V、O、Cですが、それに様々な修飾語が付けられると、文が難しく見えてきます。文の骨組み（基本構造）を、修飾語と区別して見分ける力をつけると、文が易しく見えます。

次の文章は、すべて同じ基本構造から成っています。

① The man drank wine.　基本構造は man + drank + wine.

② The Japanese man on the American ship drank wine for the first time.
基本構造は man + drank + wine.

③ The Japanese man who had been shipwrecked and saved by the American ship drank something red that looked like human blood for the first time in his life.
基本構造は man + drank + something.

このように、文を複雑に見せているのは、修飾語です。

2. 修飾語には、形容詞的修飾語と副詞的修飾語の2種類があります。

2-1 形容詞的修飾語には、（ア）形容詞、（イ）形容詞句、（ウ）形容詞節、があります。

（ア）形容詞　　　　the young man

（イ）形容詞句　　　the man on the ship

　　　　　　　　　　the man fishing in the sea

　　　　　　　　　　the man saved by the American ship

　　※「句」とは、全体として一つのまとまった意味を持つ語群のことです。

（ウ）形容詞節　　　the man who was saved by the American ship

※「節」とは、全体として一つのまとまった意味を持つ語群で、その中に S ＋ V を持つもののことです。

2-2 副詞的修飾語には、（エ）副詞、（オ）副詞句、（カ）副詞節、があります。

（エ）副詞　　　　The ship will arrive tomorrow.

（オ）副詞句　　　The ship will arrive on Monday.

（カ）副詞節　　　The ship will arrive after the storm is gone.

　　　　　　　　The ship will arrive when the clock strikes eleven.

3. 修飾語は、被修飾語のできるだけ近くに置かれます。英文を読む時は、このことを覚えて読みましょう。英文を作る際にも、修飾語は被修飾語の直近に置くようにしましょう。

発見学習-1

　既に習った文章を使って、修飾語と文の骨組みを区別して読む練習をしましょう。次の文では、骨組みは大きな字で、修飾語は小さな字で書かれています。スピードを持って、大きな字だけを拾い読みをしてみましょう。こうした読み方があなたの読書スピード増につながります。

Do you know the **story** of Robinson Crusoe?

This **story was based** on a real person.

His **name was Alexander Selkirk**, a sailor on a cargo ship.

While sailing, **Alexander felt** that the **ship was** not **safe** enough.

It had a bad **water leak.**

One day, the **ship stopped** at a small uninhabited island.

Alexander asked his **captain** to **repair the ship**.

But the **captain refused** to do so.

So, **Alexander chose** to **stay** on the island rather than sail on the dangerous ship.

The **captain agreed** and **left him** on the island – a lonely island in the Pacific Ocean 670 kilometers from Chile.

Alexander **had** only a few **tools** and the **Bible**.

He caught wild **goats** for meat and **ate** wild **vegetables**.

So **food** and **shelter was not** a serious **problem** for him.

But **he suffered** enormously from loneliness.

Four years later, **Alexander was rescued** by the ship.

He returned to his home in England.

He found his **life** there too **busy**.

He even **missed** the **loneliness** of the old uninhabited island.

Every **language has** its own **way** of addressing people.

For example, in Japanese, **you must use** *sonkei-go*, that is, honorific language, when you speak to your superiors.

Also, **you cannot call** your **superiors** by their first name;

you must call them by their surname, adding '-san' after it.

Now, **I will give you** a **quiz**.

Imagine your boss is Ichiro Suzuki.

What **can you call him** – 'Ichiro', 'Ichiro-san', 'Suzuki', or 'Suzuki-san'?

The correct **answer is 'Suzuki-san'** .

However, '**Ichiro-san' can be okay** if you two are friends and having a private conversation.

How about in English?

When you meet a person for the first time, **it is safe** to call the person by his or her surname, putting 'Mr.' or 'Miss' before it.

For example, when you meet Linda Brown for the first time, **you should call her 'Miss Brown'.**

Very often, the other **person will say**, "**You can call me** by my first name."

or "**Call me Linda**."

Then, **you can call each other** by the your first names.

次の文の中で、下線部はその直前の語を修飾する修飾語です。そして、その全部が同じ基本構造でできています。それは、どのような構造（品詞と品詞の組み合わせ）で出来ているでしょうか？

Every language has its own way of addressing people. <u>For example</u>, <u>in Japanese</u>, you must use *sonkei-go*, that is, honorific language, when you speak <u>to your superiors</u>. Also, you cannot call your superiors <u>by their first name</u>; you must call them <u>by their surname</u>, adding '-san' <u>after it</u>.

Now, I will give you a quiz. Imagine you are working <u>for a company</u> and your boss is Ichiro Suzuki. What can you call him--'Ichiro', 'Ichiro-san', 'Suzuki', or 'Suzuki-san'? The correct answer is 'Suzuki-san' . However, 'Ichiro-san' can be okay if you two are friends and having a private conversation.

How about <u>in English</u>? When you meet a person <u>for the first time</u>, it is safe to call the person <u>by his or her surname</u>, putting 'Mr.' or 'Miss' <u>before it</u>. <u>For example</u>, when you meet Linda Brown, you should call her 'Miss Brown'. Then, very often, the other person will say, "You can call me <u>by my first name</u>." or "Call me Linda." Then, you can call each other <u>by your first names</u>.

なお、この形をした修飾語は、英文に非常に多く出現します。

学習上のヒント

修飾語が入り組んで文の骨組みが見えにくい時は、次のようにすると解りやすくなります。

１．長い修飾語をカッコにくくってみる。

（例）The Japanese man **(**who had been saved by the American ship**)** drank wine for the first time.

２．文の骨組みだけを一行目に残し、修飾語を２行目以降に降ろす。

（例）The Japanese man   drank wine.

    who had been saved by the American ship   for the first time

＊修飾語は、下記の例のように、下へ下へと書き降ろしていくことが可能です。これを見ると、修飾語がどれだけ複雑に重なり合っているかがわかりますね。しかし、このような分析はあくまでも自分の

英文理解の補助に留めて、微細な分析は必要ありません。

（微細な分析の例）

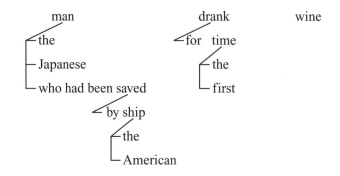

　英語には、pp. 42-43 の（イ）（ウ）（エ）（オ）（カ）のように、後置修飾（後ろの修飾語が前の語を修飾する場合）が多く用いられます。こうした文を語順訳する時には、次のようにするとよいでしょう。

（語順訳例）

The Japanese man/ <u>who</u> had been shipwrecked/ and saved by the American ship/
その日本人　　　 / <u>その人</u>は難破して　　　 / 　アメリカ船に救助されていた /
drank something red　 / <u>that</u> looked like human blood　　 / for the first time in his life..
何か赤いものを飲んだ / <u>それは</u>人間の血のように見えた / それは人生で初めてのことだった

　上の訳の下線部に着目してください。この文脈では 'who' を「その人は」、'that' を「それは」と訳すことで、すんなりと語順どおりに訳していけます。

参考文：This is the House that Jack Built Song

　英語は、基本構造は単純です。しかしそれに修飾語が付き、その修飾語に更に修飾語が付き、またそれに修飾語が付くことで、複雑化してゆきます。ちょうど、心棒に粘土を貼り付け、その粘土の上に更に粘土を貼り付け、重ねていく、粘土細工に似ています。次のナーサリーライム（英国の伝統的な子どもの遊び歌）はその典型例です。

　この歌では、上の行から下の行へと、次々と修飾語が重ねられていきます。［S＋V］の構造から言えば、14重の構造をしています。こんな複雑な歌を、逆戻り訳で日本語にするのは不可能に近いでしょう。しかし、語順訳ならば下記のように簡単にできます。

This is the House that Jack Built Song 🔊

(HooplaKidz Nursery Rhymes & Kids Songs より)

(https://www.youtube.com/watch?v=7sDSYVfnj_E)

This is the horse and the hound and the horn	これが、その馬と猟犬と角笛だ
that belonged to the farmer	それらはお百姓さんのもので、
sowing his corn	お百姓さんは麦の種をまいていた
that kept the cock	それは雄鶏を飼うための麦で
that crowed in the morn	その雄鶏は朝に鳴き
that woke the priest all shaven and shorn	それがつるつる頭のお坊さんを起こし
that married the man all tattered and torn	その坊さんがボロを着た男を結婚させた
that kissed the maiden all forlorn	その男は身寄りのない乙女にキスをし
that milked the cow with the crumpled horn	その乙女は角の曲がった雌牛の乳をしぼり
that tossed the dog	その角が犬を放り上げた
that worried the cat	その犬は猫を困らせていて
that chased the rat	その猫はネズミを追いかけた
that ate the malt	そのネズミは麦芽を食べた
that lay in the house	その麦芽はその家にしまってあった
that Jack built.	その家をジャックが建てた。

Unit 6A

英問英答に答える秘訣

英語の検定試験や面接試験では、書かれた passage や受験者本人について、英語の質問に英語で答える問題がよく出題されます。いわゆる「英問英答」問題です。

英問英答では、求められる情報を探し出す力と、見つけた情報を適切な英文で答える力が試されます。

たとえば面接試験で、

"How do you commute to school?" という質問に対して、

（ア）"By train." と答えるのと、

（イ）"I commute by train." と答えるのとでは、情報は同じですが丁寧さが違います。もしも面接試験を通して、（ア）のような簡略化した返事ばかりをするとしたら、面接員はその人をぞんざいな人だと感じることでしょう。家族や親しい友人との間で（ア）のような言葉使いをするのはもちろん良いですが、面接試験や公開討論などの公の場でもそのような言葉使いをする人は、公私の区別のできない人と思われかねません。そこでこの Unit では、ややあらたまった場面での英語の質問への答え方を勉強することにします。

英語の質問に適切な英文で答える秘訣は、相手の質問の文構造［S（主部）と V（述語動詞）］と同じ文構造を使って答えることです。

"How do you commute to school?" と聞かれたら、その［S］+［V］を使って

"I commute by train." と答えればいいのです。

発見学習 🔊

実はこれまでのユニットで行ってきた英問英答で、皆さんは既にその実例にたくさん接してきています。下記にそれを羅列してあります。例にならって、それぞれ質問と応答の文の S と V をマークしてみましょう。

Unit 1A:

（例）Which city did German airplanes attack during World War II? – They attacked London.

① What did German airplanes drop on the city of London? – They dropped many

---

bombs.

② What hit the department store one night? – A bomb hit the department store.

③ Who was injured by the bombing? – Fortunately, nobody was injured.

④ What was damaged by the bombing? – The department store was damaged.

⑤ Was the store open the next morning? – Yes, it was.

⑥ What did the big sign say? – It said 'More Open'.

Unit 1B:

① Who was Robinson Crusoe? – He was the hero of a novel.

② What was Alexander Selkirk? – He was a sailor.

③ What was the name of his ship? – It was Cinque Ports.

④ Why did Alexander think his ship was dangerous? – Because it had a bad water leak.

⑤ Why did Alexander choose to stay on the island? – Because he thought it was safer than his ship.

⑥ Did anybody else live on the island? – No, they didn't.

⑦ What was Alexander's biggest problem on the island? – It was loneliness.

⑧ How long did he stay on the island? – He stayed there for four years.

Unit 3:

① What does 'sonkei-go' mean in English? – It means honorific language.

② When is the honorific language used in Japanese? – It is used when we speak to our superiors.

③ Do people usually call their boss by his/her first name in Japan? – No, we don't.

④ Imagine you are meeting a person named Mike Harvey for the first time. What will you call him – Mike, Harvey, or Mr. Harvey? – I will call him Mr. Harvey.

Unit 4A:

① How many people live in the whole world? – About 7.3 billion people live in the world.

② How many people speak English as their native language? – About 380 million people do.

③ How many people speak English as a second or foreign language? – About 1.12 billion people do.

④ Is English spoken mainly as a native language in the world? – No, it isn't.

⑤ Is English spoken mainly as a second or a foreign language in the world? – Yes, it is.

⑥ What kind of English speakers will be the major speech partners for Japanese people in the future? – They will be non-native speakers of English from other countries.

Unit 4B:

① What is a good way to start talking with new people in a relaxed manner? – It is to have small talk.

② What topics do people usually choose for small talk? – They usually choose casual topics such as weather, food, and sports.

③ How can we make our conversation interactive? – We make sure that each of us has equal time to speak and listen to each other, like playing tennis.

Unit 5A:

① Has Junya got a job at Texas Barbecue House? – Yes, he has.

② Who is the manager of the Texas Barbecue House? – Barbara is.

③ How long has Texas Barbecue House been open? – It has been open for ten years.

④ Why can't the customer pay for the lunch? – Because she has lost her wallet.

進行形と現在分詞

1. 動詞に〜ing が付いた形には、2 種類の異なる働きがあります：

①現在分詞（「〜している」）I am study<u>ing</u> English now.

②動名詞（「〜すること」）My hobby is paint<u>ing</u> pictures.

ルール：〜ing 形には 2 種類ある	
現在分詞	動名詞
I am **painting** a picture now. 意味：「〜している」 ↑ 今回	My hobby is **painting** pictures. 意味：「〜すること」

この Unit では、①現在分詞を学習します。

2. 現在分詞は、次の 2 つの用法に使われます。

（1）進行形を作る

　　（例）The sun is <u>shining</u> brightly.

　　（進行形の形）be 動詞 + 現在分詞

　　（進行形の意味）「〜している」（まだその動作が終わっていない）

（2）現在分詞の形容詞的用法

　　（例）Look at the <u>sleeping</u> cat. / Look at the cat <u>sleeping under the car</u>.

　　（形）現在分詞 1 語の時は、名詞の前に置かれて、その名詞を修飾する。

　　　　 2 語以上の時は、名詞の後に置かれて、その名詞を修飾する。

　　（意味）「眠っているネコ」 / 「車の下で眠っているネコ」

現在分詞の2用法

進行形を作る ［be 動詞 + 〜ing］	前後の名詞を修飾する （形容詞的用法）
(a) The cat is sleeping. そのネコは眠っている。 （現在進行形）	a sleeping cat 眠っているネコ
(b) The cat was climbing a tree. そのネコは木に登っていた。 （過去進行形）	a cat sleeping on the sofa ソファの上で眠っているネコ
(c) The cat will be eating some fish. そのネコは魚を食べているだろう。 （未来進行形）	

長文：The Woodcutter and Three Axes

Vocabulary Hints: 次の 1〜14 の語の説明を、下の a〜n から選んで補いなさい。🔊

1. woodcutter	（名）	2. honest	（形）	3. axe	（名）
4. breeze	（名）	5. spring	（名）	6. splash	（名）
7. bubble	（動）	8. goddess	（名）	9. brilliantly	（副）
10. iron	（名）	11. humble	（形）	12. exactly	（副）
13. honesty	（名）	14. conclude	（動）		

説明

a. 鉄	b. 女神	c. まさしく	d. 泉	e. ざぶんという水音
f. 正直な	g. 謙虚な	h. 泡立つ	i. そよ風	j. きらきらと
k. finish	l. a man who cuts trees	m. the quality of being honest		n. a tool for cutting woods

練習-1

　次の文章は、よく知られた「木こりと3本の斧」の物語です。物語内の（　　　）内の語を進行形（be 動詞＋動詞の ing 形）にしなさい。

内容理解 🔊

1．女神は、木こりのどういうところに感激したのでしょう？

2．女神が木こりにくれた贈り物は何でしょう？

3．女神と出会って後、木こりの生活に変化はありましたか？

(1)

Once upon a time, there lived a woodcutter in a little village. He was a very honest man. One day, he (cut) trees in the forest with his big axe. The sun (shine) brightly in the sky. A nice breeze (blow) through the trees. Birds (sing) here and there. The woodcutter (sing) happily as he worked.

But suddenly, his hands slipped, and his axe flew into the air. It flew and fell into the spring near-by.

"Splash!"

"Oh, my God! My axe! My axe! I cannot work without my axe! What shall I do?"

The woodcutter shook his head and walked around the spring. But the spring was so deep that he could not see his axe.

Then suddenly, a beautiful woman came up from the bubbling water. She (wear) golden clothes shining brightly. She was the goddess of the spring. She (hold) an axe in her hands – a golden axe shining brilliantly in the sun. "Woodcutter, is this your axe?" asked the goddess. "No, it isn't. That axe is gold, but mine is iron," said the woodcutter. "Oh, you humble man! You could buy 100 iron axes with this gold axe, " she said. The goddess went back into the water.

After a few minutes, the goddess came up from the water again. This time she (hold) a silver axe in her hands. "Woodcutter, is this your axe?" asked the goddess. "No, it isn't. That axe is silver, but mine is iron," said the woodcutter. "Oh, what a humble man! You could buy 20 iron axes with this silver axe," she said, and went back into the water.

(2)

After a few minutes, the goddess came up from the water again. This time she (hold) an old iron axe in her hands. "Woodcutter, is this your axe?" asked the goddess. "Yes, it is! It's exactly MY axe," said the woodcutter happily. The goddess smiled and gave him the iron axe. Then she went back into the spring, and came back with the golden and silver axes in her hands. "Woodcutter, you have made me very happy with your honesty. I will give you these axes as a present. Stay honest all through your life."

Six months have passed since then. The woodcutter is working in the forest as before. The sun (shine) in the sky. Birds (sing) happily in the trees. A cool and nice breeze (blow) through the trees. Nothing has changed. What about the golden and silver axes? – How would you conclude this story ?

今回からは、穴埋め式ではなく、自分の力で答の文を組み立てましょう。

(1) When the woodcutter was working in the forest, something bad happened. What happened?

(2) Was the woodcutter able to find his axe in the spring water?

(3) When the goddess came out of the water for the first time, what did she have in her hands?

(4) When the goddess came out of the water for the second time, what did she have in her hands?

(5) When the goddess came out of the water for the third time, what did she have in her hands?

(6) Why did the goddess give him the gold and silver axes, too?

発見学習

上の物語には、現在分詞の形容詞的用法が3回出て来ます。その箇所を指摘しなさい。

課題

上の物語を、あなたならどのように完結させますか？最後の "How would you conclude this story?" の問いに応えて、締めくくりの英文を書いてみよう。

Unit 7

受動態と過去分詞

ルール

1. 受動態の形は be 動詞＋過去分詞、意味は「〜される」

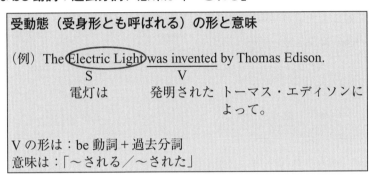

> 受動態（受身形とも呼ばれる）の形と意味
>
> （例）The Electric Light was invented by Thomas Edison.
>   S   V
>   電灯は   発明された　トーマス・エディソンに
>   よって。
>
> V の形は：be 動詞＋過去分詞
> 意味は：「〜される／〜された」

2. 過去分詞は動詞の変化形の 1 つ、Unit 5A で学習済み。

3. 受動態の否定文・疑問文の作り方：V が be 動詞の文と同じ作り方です（Unit 1B）。

平叙文　Carrying a gun is prohibited in Japan.
　　　　銃の携帯は日本では禁止されている。

否定文　Carrying a gun is (not) prohibited in America.
　　　　銃の携帯はアメリカでは禁止されていない。

疑問文　Is carrying a gun prohibited in your country?
　　　　あなたの国では、銃の携帯は禁止されていますか？

4. 受動態の文に助動詞を加える方法：V の前に助動詞を加える。

The next Olympics (will) are held in this country.
　　　　　　　　　　　　↓
　　　　　　　　　　be（原形）

次のオリンピック大会はこの国で開かれるでしょう。

5. 英文では、能動態が基本です。受動態が好まれるのは下記の場合だけです：

（ア）主語の流れを自然にするため、

That restaurant is my favorite. It's called "Jimmy's." （Unit 15、ルール 5 参照）

（イ）動作を受ける方が情報として重要である場合、

Prof. Honjo was awarded Nobel Prize in 2018 (by the Nobel Committee).

この情報に重点

（ウ）その動作を起こした者が不明、あるいは、言いたくない場合

Three girls have been kidnapped.

6. 過去分詞の形容詞的用法

be 動詞が前に付いていない過去分詞は、「～された」という意味を持ち、形容詞と同じ働きをします。

（例）　imported beef　輸入された牛肉　（過去分詞 1 語の場合、前から後ろを修飾する）

beef imported from Australia　オーストラリアから輸入された牛肉（過去分詞の語群の場合、後ろから前を修飾する）

長文：How People on the Bus Survived

Vocabulary Hints: 次の 1～14 の語の説明を、下の a～n から選んで補いなさい。 🔊

1. charter	（動）	2. flood	（動）	3. passenger	（名）
4. elderly	（形）	5. traffic	（名）	6. paralyze	（動）
7. rose（rise）	（動）	8. tightly	（副）	9. enormously	（副）
10. encourage	（動）	11. SDF	（名）	12. cooperation	（名）
13. entitle	（動）	14. submerge	（動）		

説明

a. 交通	b. 励ます	c. 堅く	d. ～という題を付ける
e. 麻痺させる	f. old	g. overflow	h. working together for a purpose
i. hire for private use		j. greatly	k. put under the water
l. people who travel in a vehicle		m. moved upwards	n. 自衛隊

1．そのバスにはどのような客が乗っていましたか？
2．そのバスはなぜ立ち往生したのですか？
3．乗客と運転手はどこに避難しましたか？
4．絶望しかけた彼らを、何が励ましたのですか？
5．彼らはどのようにして救助されましたか？

On October 20, 2004,/ a chartered bus was driving/ along the country road in Maizuru-shi, Kyoto-fu. On that day,/ Western Japan was hit/ by a very big typhoon. A near-by river flooded,/ and the road was covered with water.

There were 37 passengers on the bus. They were a group of elderly people/ from Hyogo-ken. Because of the flood,/ the traffic was paralyzed/ on the road. The water came into the bus,/ rose higher and higher,/ and reached the seats on the bus. The passengers decided to get out of the bus/ and climb on to the roof of the bus.

Thirty-seven people and the bus driver/ got on the roof of the bus/ – in the darkness,/ in the strong wind,/ under the heavy rain. Finally,/ the water rose above the bus roof. People's feet and knees were covered/ with the flood waters. They were shaking/ from the cold and fear. Many of them thought/ that they were going to die before long.

Suddenly,/ somebody started singing a familiar song,/ *Uewo Muite Aruko*. Some people joined,/ and soon all the people were singing loudly. They held each other's shoulders and arms tightly/ so that they would not be washed away/ by the water. They were enormously encouraged/ by the singing.

Around 5 a.m., after about 10 hours,/ the bus was discovered/ by an SDF helicopter. One by one, /the people were lifted up/ into the helicopter. No life was lost,/ thanks to the cooperation/ of the people on the bus.

Later,/ this story was published/ in a book/ entitled '*Bus Suibotsu Jiko--Shiawasewo Kureta Jujikan*' (*The Submerged Bus – the Ten Hours That Gave Us Happiness*) /from Asahi Shuppan.

（注：SDF = Self Defence Force）

Answer these questions in English.

（1） Who was traveling on the bus?

（2） How did they feel when they stood on the roof of the bus?

（3） How many hours did they stand on the roof of the bus?

（4） What was the weather like while they stood on the bus roof?

（5） What did they do to stay alive on the roof?

（6） What encouraged the people on the bus roof?

（7） Who discovered the submerged bus?

（8） How were they saved?

（9） How many people were killed in this bus accident?

（10） How did you feel when you read this story?

発見学習

１．上の文中の受動態（be 動詞＋過去分詞）を 二重下線 でマークしなさい。

２．上の文中の過去分詞の形容詞的用法を波線でマークしなさい。

語順訳

次の文を語順訳しなさい。

（1） A near-by river flooded,/ and the road was covered with water.

（2） People's feet and knees were covered/ with flood waters.

（3） They held each other's shoulders and arms tightly/ so that they would not be

washed away/ by the water.

（4） Later,/ this story was published/ in a book/ entitled ‘*Bus Suibotsu Jiko--*

Shiawasewo Kureta Jujikan’.

Unit 8

不定詞

1. 不定詞は言葉のパッケージのようなもの

（例）

Do you like	songs?		Yes, I like	songs.
あなたは好きですか	歌が		はい、私は好きです	歌が

Do you like	to sing ?		Yes, I like	to sing .
あなたは好きですか	歌うことが		はい、私は好きです	歌うことが
			I like	to sing in karaoke .
			私は好きです	カラオケで歌うことが

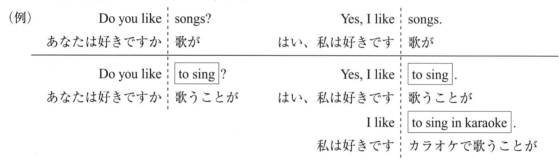

Do＋you＋like＋ パッケージ ?

上の☐で囲まれた語群は、段ボール箱に詰めた荷物のように、1つの単語のように働きます。どのような文脈で使われても、その中身は変化しません。

2. 不定詞の形：[to＋動詞の原形]

不定詞の意味：

(1)「～すること」 To have an exercise is good for your health.

　　名詞的用法 （ 運動すること はあなたの健康に良い）

(2)「～するために」（目的） My mother works hard to support my family .

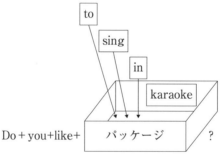

　　副詞的用法 （私の母は 家族を養うために 一生懸命働く）

(3) 「〜したために」（原因） I am glad to see you here .

　　　 ┄┄┄┄┄┄┄
　　　 ┊ 副詞的用法 ┊　（ ここであなたに会えて うれしいです）
　　　 ┄┄┄┄┄┄┄

(4) 「〜するための」 I am hungry. I want something to eat .

　　　 ┄┄┄┄┄┄┄
　　　 ┊ 形容詞的用法 ┊　（私は何か 食べる ものが欲しい）
　　　 ┄┄┄┄┄┄┄

長文：Complimenting

Vocabulary Hints: 次の 1〜7 の語の説明を、下の a〜g から選んで補いなさい。 ◀))

1. praise	（動）	2. lubricant	（名）	3. strengthen	（動）
4. excellent	（形）	5. respond	（動）	6. add	（動）
7. additional	（形）				

説明

| a. 潤滑油 | b. 強める | c. 付け加える | d. 誉める | e. 追加の |
| f. answer | g. very good indeed | | | |

内容理解 ◀))

1．英語文化では、他人を誉めることには、どういう効果がありますか？
2．何かを誉められた時には、どのように返事をしたらよいでしょうか？

　How many times did you compliment other people during the last week? 'To compliment' means to praise someone.

　To compliment others is very common and important in American culture. Complimenting is an important social lubricant there. It is an effective and safe way to start a friendly conversation with other people, even with strangers. Also, Americans frequently give compliments to their own family members to strengthen their love. My American friend says he gives at least one compliment a day to his family members.

　Here are some expressions to compliment other people.

(a) 外見（Physical Appearance）： *"You look very nice in that shirt."*

(b) 人柄（Personality）： *"You have a wonderful sense of humor."*

（c）家族（Family Member）：*"Your children are so well-mannered."*

（d）能力（Abilities）：*"This is my student Melinda. I am proud of her."*

（e）業績（Achievements）：*"You did an excellent job."*

（f）所持品（Belongings）：*"I like your T-shirt."*

（g）食事（Meals）：*"I love this meal. You're a very good cook."*

When someone compliments you, respond with "Thank you," and add a piece of additional information. Here is an example:

Friend: *I like your earrings.*

You: *Thanks, they were a present from my mother.*

英問英答 🔊

Answer these questions in English.

（1）How can we start a friendly conversation safely with a stranger in English?

（2）Why do American people frequently give compliments to their family members?

（3）How do people usually respond to a compliment given to them?

（4）What do people usually give compliments about?

（5）What do you think about the American culture of complimenting as a social lubricant?

語順訳

次の文を語順訳しなさい。

（1）To compliment others/ is very common and important/ in American culture.

（2）Complimenting is an effective and safe way/ to start a friendly conversation/

with other people,/ even with strangers.

発見学習

課題 1. 上の文中の不定詞を見つけ出し、下線を引きなさい。

課題 2. それぞれの不定詞は、上記（1）〜（4）のどの意味を表していますか？

ルール 2

1. 不定詞と「誰が？」

（1）通常は、不定詞に表された行動を行う人は、その文の S（主部）である。

　①My father wants to buy a new car.　誰が buy するか？→ my father が

　②I would like to come home early tonight.　誰が come home するか？→ I が

（2）不定詞の行動を行うのが、主部とは別の人の時は、次の例のように表現する。

　①I want my father to buy a new car.　誰が buy するか？→ my father が

　②I would like you to come home early tonight.　誰が come home するか？→ you が

2. 不定詞の否定形

　「〜しないこと」「〜しないために」「〜しないための」は、［not＋to＋動詞の原形］で表す。

　＊「決して〜しない」は［never＋to＋動詞の原形］

練習

次の文が日本文と同じ内容を表すように、適切な個所に not を入れて文を完成しなさい。

（1）They decided to buy the house.

　　彼らはその家を買わないことに決めた。

（2）I promise to tell anyone the secret.

　　私はその秘密を誰にも言わないことを約束する。

（3）　She asked me to call her again.

彼女は私に、もう二度と電話し<u>ない</u>ようにと言った。

3. 不定詞と形式主語

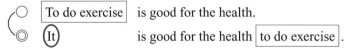

　英語は、長い主部を嫌います。→長い主部を後ろに回して、→代わりに、It という仮の主部を置きます。

　上の例では、下の文の方が好まれます。

Unit 9

動名詞

Unit 6B では、[動詞＋ing] 形の現在進行形を学びました。この Unit では、同じく [動詞＋ing] の形をした動名詞を学びます。まずは例文を見てみましょう。

例 1： My hobby | is | singing . （私の趣味は歌うことです。）（singing が文中の補語になる）
       S   V   C

例 2： Singing | makes | me | happy. （歌うことは私を幸せにします。）
       S   V   O   C   （singing が文中の主部になる）

例 3： I | enjoy | singing with my college choir . （私は大学の合唱クラブで歌うことを楽しみます）
      S V   O   （singing が文中の目的語になる）

ルール

1. 動詞なのに、名詞の働きをするので「動名詞」と呼びます。動名詞を作るには、動詞の原形に ing を付け足せばよいのです。

2. **動名詞は、前置詞の目的語にもなります。**

               （前置詞）   （動名詞）
Our President is | against | importing foreign products | .
我が国の大統領は外国製品輸入に反対です。

               （前置詞）   （動名詞）
Wash your hands | before | eating meals | .   食事を食べる前には手を洗いなさい。

3. Unit 6B と 9 のまとめ

これまで習ったことを整理しましょう。[動詞＋〜ing] 形には、次の（ア）（イ）（ウ）の 3 種類があります。

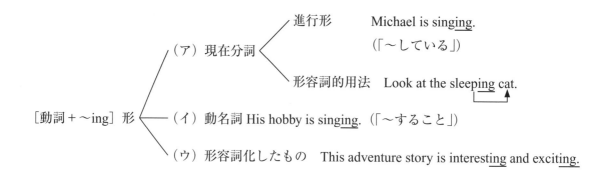

	進行形	Michael is singing.
		（「〜している」）
（ア）現在分詞		
	形容詞的用法	Look at the sleeping cat.

［動詞＋〜ing］形 ──── （イ）動名詞 His hobby is singing.（「〜すること」）

（ウ）形容詞化したもの　This adventure story is interesting and exciting.

長文：What Is the Best Way to Learn English?

内容理解 ◀))

1．Part 1：英語が使えるようになるための最良の方法とは、何だと言っていますか？
　　　　　　本来の目的のために英語を使うと、どのようなメリットがありますか？
　　　　　　もしもネット上の友達募集サイトを使うとしたら、その際の注意点は何ですか？
2．Part 2：言語はどのようにして効率的に習得できると述べていますか？
　　　　　　言語学習では、どのような難易度の文章を聞き・読むのが理想的だと述べていますか？
3．Part 3：英語授業での成績は良いのに、英語が話せない主な原因は何だと書かれていますか？
　　　　　　英語で自分の考えを述べる力を育てるためには、どのような方法がありますか？

Part 1

Vocabulary Hints: 次の 1〜13 の語の説明を、下の a〜m から選んで補いなさい。◀))

1. single	（形）	2. purpose	（名）	3. interaction	（名）
4. sense of achievement		5. self-confidence	（名）	6. arrange	（動）
7. caution	（名）	8. romantic	（形）	9. disguise	（動）
10. identity	（名）	11. marital status		12. screen	（動）
13. function	（名）				

説明

a. 婚姻状況	b. 恋愛の	c. さえぎる	d. 自信	e. 身分
f. ごまかす	g. 機能	h. 目的	i. 達成感	j. warning
k. only one	l. make plans	m. communication		

1 My students often ask me, "What
2 is the best way to learn to speak
3 English?" My answer to this
4 question is:

5 There is not a single best way to
6 learn English. There are several
7 good ways, and you can choose
8 from among them. Now, I will tell
9 you some of the ways to learn
10 English effectively and for free.

11

12 **Use English for a real purpose.**

13 Have you ever used English for a
14 real purpose? For instance, to help
15 a foreigner on the street, to
16 exchange E-mails with a non-
17 Japanese speaker, or to make some
18 business interaction with a
19 foreigner?

20 Using English for a real purpose
21 is exciting. You will get a sense of
22 achievement when you have
(1)
23 succeeded in communicating in
24 English, and it will add to your self-
25 confidence.

26 You don't have any foreign
27 friends to communicate with?

28 That's no problem. Get one of your
29 Japanese friends and arrange to talk
30 with her/him in English at a certain
31 time of the day. For example,
32 arrange to talk with one of your
33 friends on the phone from 8 to 8:10
34 p.m., or exchange English E-mails
35 once every day.

36 If you want to find a foreign
37 Email friend, you might try online
38 sites such as *Interpals Penpals*
39 (https://www.interpals.net/). It is a
40 website where you can find people
41 all over the world looking for Email
42 friends. However, here is a word of
43 caution: Some of the members of
44 friend-finding sites are only looking
45 for a romantic relationship. And some
46 may be disguising their identity,
47 such as their age, marital status,
48 job, and even sex. So use its contact
49 screening functions to prevent such
50 contact. Also, do not give your
51 online friends your personal
52 information such as your full name,
53 mail address, phone number, school
54 name, or home address.

Part 2

Vocabulary Hints: 次の 1〜9 の語の説明を、下の a〜i から選んで補いなさい。🔊

1. acquire	(動)	2. input	(名)	3. present	(形)
4. pleasure	(名)	5. material	(名)	6. narrate	(動)
7. instructive	(形)	8. Aesop	(名)	9. comprehension	(名)

説明

a. 理解	b. 教材	c. イソップ	d. 入力	e. 読み上げる
f. learn	g. feeling of enjoyment	h. existing now	i. giving useful information	

1 **Read and listen to a lot of easy**
2 **English.**
3　　Another way to learn English
4 effectively is to read and listen to a
5 lot of easy English stories and
6 essays. For example, *Spotlight*
7 *English Listening* (https://
8 spotlightenglish.com/) offers more
9 than a hundred listening stories for
10 beginners. They are narrated rather
11 slowly, and the stories are
12 interesting and instructive.
13　　(2) According to recent studies,
14 language is best acquired through
15 understanding plenty of meaningful
16 language input. How easy should
17 the reading materials be? They
18 should be just a little above your
19 present level. Then, you can
20 understand them easily without
21 using a dictionary. You can enjoy

22 understanding them smoothly, and
23 will find more and more pleasure in
24 listening to or reading English.
25　　Now, where can you find those
26 easy materials? If you go to a large
27 bookstore, you will find some easy
28 graded readers for English learners.
29 Your college library might have a
30 collection of such books. You can
31 also find them on the Internet.
32 *Jaremaga* is an online mail
33 magazine in easy English which
34 you can subscribe to for free
35 (catchawave.jp/jm/). *Aesop's*
36 *Collection Online* (http://www.
37 aesopfables.com/) offers more than
38 200 easy stories to read. *My English*
39 *Pages* (https://www.
40 myenglishpages.com/site_php_
41 files/reading.php) contains about
42 200 reading stories of a little higher

43 level. It also gives comprehension
44 quizzes for each story, which helps

45 you check your comprehension.

Part 3

Vocabulary Hints: 次の 1〜11 の語の説明を、下の a〜k から選んで補いなさい。 🔊

1. self-talk	(名)	2. pastime	(名)	3. memorable	(形)
4. nuclear	(形)	5. generation	(名)	6. achieve	(動)
7. draft	(名)	8. solution	(名)	9. switch	(動)
10. intelligently	(副)	11. spontaneously	(副)		

説明

a. 自分との対話	b. 知的に	c. 原稿	d. 原子力の	e. 解決策
f. 即興的に	g. change	h. recreation	i. succeed in fulfilling	
j. unforgettable	k. production of energy			

1 **Self-talk or Keep a Diary in**
2 **English.**
3 　"What is your favorite pastime?"
4 "What is the most memorable event
5 in your life?" "What do you think
6 about nuclear power generation?"
7 "What do you want to achieve while
8 you are in college?" Can you
9 answer these questions in English
10 without preparing a draft
11 beforehand? A lot of people cannot
12 speak English, not because of their
13 lack of English ability, but because
14 of their lack of ideas to discuss.

15 　Then, how can we develop our
16 own ideas to discuss in English?
17 The solution is to build the habit of
18 talking to yourself in English and
19 keeping an English diary. Find
20 some free time and switch your
21 self-talk from Japanese to English.
22 Put down your opinions about
23 recent events in your notebook or
24 smart phone in English. By doing
25 these things, you will develop the
26 habit of thinking in English. And
27 this will help you speak intelligently
28 and spontaneously in English.

Answer these questions in English.

---

(1) What kind of input is more effective for learning a language – a small amount of very difficult input, or plenty of input that is a little above our present level?

(2) Do all the people show their true identity when they appear on social networking services such as Twitter and Instagram?

(3) Some learners get high scores in English language examinations, but cannot express themselves well in English. Why does this happen?

(4) What can we do to develop our own ideas to discuss in English?

(5) How can we develop the habit of thinking in English?

語順訳

次の文を語順訳しなさい。

---

(1) You will get a sense of achievement/ when you have succeeded/ in

communicating in English,/ and it will add to your self-confidence.

(2) It is a website/ where you can find/ people all over the world/ looking for Email

friends.

(3) According to recent studies,/ language is best acquired/ through understanding/

plenty of meaningful language input.

---

(4)　A lot of people cannot speak English,/ not because of their lack of English

ability,/ but because of their lack of ideas to discuss.

発見学習

　上の文中の〜ing 形を全てマークし、それを（ア）現在分詞、（イ）動名詞、に分類しなさい。
（ただし、文中の（1）exciting と（2）interesting は、既に形容詞として出来上がってしまった語
なので、マークしなくてよろしい）

Unit 10

名詞節

ルール

1. 英文には、[S + V] の組合わせが 2 重・3 重に存在することがあります。こういう重層構造の文を「複文」と呼びます。([S + V] の組合わせが 1 重の文は「単文」と呼びます)

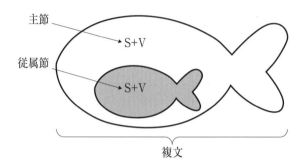

2. 重層構造の文で、大きい方の [S + V] から成る部分を「主節」、小さい方の [S + V] から成る部分を「従属節」と呼びます。

3. 従属節で、一つの名詞と同じように働くものを「名詞節」と呼びます。

4. **名詞節の例**（斜体字の部分が名詞節）

   (1) The news *that Japan won in the World Cup* is true.
   日本がワールドカップの試合で勝ったというニュースは　本当です

   (2) *What the newspaper says about the rugby team* is true.
   そのラグビー部について新聞が書いていることは　本当です

   (3) I think *that Japan will win in the World Cup.*
   私は思います　日本がワールドカップの試合で勝つだろうと
   ＊この that は、「〜ということ」と訳し、名詞節（that + S + V）を作る代表的な接続詞です。ただし、この that は省かれることもあります。

   (4) I don't know *how this accident happened.*
   私は知りません　どうやってこの事故が起こったのかを

（5）Please tell us　　*why you want to join our company.*

　我々に教えて下さい　　なぜあなたが当社に入りたいのかを

5. 「複文」という知識があると、どの S がどの V と結びついているかを見分けやすくなります。

　下記の文は、ピラミッドについて述べたものです。左右の語句をつなぎ合せて、意味の通る文にしなさい。

1．Why the Egyptian kings built such big pyramids	（a）does not seem true.
2．Some scholars say	（b）that the pyramids were built to display the king's power.
3．The story that the kings forced their people to work like slaves	（c）is still a mystery.

長文：How to Make a Request in English

Vocabulary Hints: 次の 1〜16 の語の説明を、下の a〜p から選んで補いなさい。🔊

1. extra	（形）	2. politeness	（名）	3. acceptable	（形）
4. imperative form		5. command	（動）	6. rude	（形）
7. imply	（動）	8. obligation	（名）	9. permission	（名）
10. direct	（動）	11. essentials	（名）	12. yield	（動）
13. eagerly	（副）	14. dare	（動）	15. assert	（動）
16. extraordinary	（形）				

説明

a. 譲る	b. 命令する	c. 余分の	d. 命令形	e. 義務
f. 許可	g. 礼儀正しさ	h. 本質的要素	i. impolite	j. 指示する
k. 勇気を出して〜する		l. 熱望して	m. suggest	n. unusual
o. 許容できる	p. speak and act in a forceful way			

🔊

1．下記英文中の（a）（b）（c）の表現は、どれも同じように使えると書かれていますか？

2．(a)の表現が適切なのは、どういう場合ですか？

3．(b)の表現が適切なのは、どういう場合ですか？

4．話し手が相手に指図をしているのは、どの表現ですか？

5．話し手が相手に許可を求めているのは、どの表現ですか？

Imagine you are staying in a youth hostel in Melbourne, Australia, during the summer vacation. Now you need to go to the post office in a hurry. You remember that Jonathan, one of your fellow guests in the hostel, has a bike. So you want to ask Jonathan to lend his bike to you. How would you say?

(a) "Jonathan, please lend me your bike."

(b) "Jonathan, will you lend me your bike?"

(c) "Jonathan, may I borrow your bike?"

These expressions, if translated into Japanese, will be almost the same. But each of them has different levels of politeness. The first phrase "please lend me your bike" is not considered very polite. It is only acceptable when you and Jonathan are good friends. Why is it? It is because "lend me" is in the imperative form – you are commanding Jonathan to lend his bike. In the English culture, equal human relationship is considered very important: it is considered rude for one person to give a command to another person.

Then how about the second expression, "Will you lend me your bike?"? "Will you---?" implies that the other person has some duty to do that for you. Therefore, it can only be polite if Jonathan has some obligation to lend you his bike.

What about the last one, "May I borrow your bike?" Yes, it sounds very polite. Its casual forms, "Can I---?" and "Could I---?" also sound polite. Why are they considered polite? The reason is that they are asking for Jonathan's permission instead of commanding or directing him. "May I" means that the decision-maker is Jonathan, not you. Respecting the other person's right to decide is one of the essentials of English politeness, and it is particularly important when making a

---

request. If you yield the decision-making right to the other person, you are considered polite.

Now you might wonder why a man in love often asks his girlfriend, "Will you marry me?" in some romantic movies. That's a good question! In this case the man wants to marry her so eagerly that he even dares to assert himself. Therefore, it is effective in such a situation. But of course you should limit such a strong expression only to extraordinary occasions.

To conclude, when making a request I recommend to use "May I", "Could I", or "Can I". Then Jonathan will consider you polite, and gladly say, "Sure, go ahead!"

英問英答 🔊

Answer these questions in English.

(1) Which is a more polite way of making a request in English, asking for permission or giving a command?

(2) What is one of the basic principles of English politeness?

(3) Why do some men in love choose less polite expressions when they propose to their girlfriends?

(4) Suppose you have got lost on the street in New York. You want to stop a passer-by and ask the way to the subway station. What will you say to him/her?

語順訳と発見学習 1

次の文中の名詞節に下線を引き、さらに全文を語順訳しなさい。

(1) Imagine / you are staying / in a youth hostel in Melbourne, Australia, / during

the summer vacation.

(2)　You remember / that Jonathan, one of your fellow guests in the hostel, / has an

extra bike.

(3)　"Will you---?" implies / that the other person / has some duty / to do that for you.

(4)　The reason is / that they are asking for Jonathan's permission / instead of

commanding or directing him.

(5)　It means / that the decision-maker is Jonathan, / not you.

(6)　You might wonder / why a man in love / often asks his girlfriend, / "Will you

marry me?" / in some romantic movies.

(7)　The man wants to marry her so eagerly / that he even dares to assert himself.

発見学習 2

　長文 'How to Make a Request in English' の中の、名詞節をみつけて、それを ［　］ で囲ってみ
よう。

次の文の、S を ◯ で囲み、V に下線を引きなさい（複文では、大きい方の SV のみを答えなさい）

（1）　These expressions, if translated into Japanese, will be almost the same.

（2）　Its casual forms, "Can I---?" and "Could I---?" also sound polite.

（3）　Respecting the other person's right to decide is one of the essentials of English-speaking politeness.

---

6. 名詞と名詞句と名詞節

英語は、様々なことを表現する方法として、名詞の代わりに名詞の代用品を使う工夫をします。

（a）My mother tells me stories.（私の母は私にお話をしてくれる）

（b）My mother teaches me how to bake bread.（私の母は私にパンの焼き方を教えてくれる）

（c）My mother tells me that I will be a good cook.

　　（私の母は私に、将来料理が上手になるだろうと言う）

上の文（b）の下線部 how to bake bread は、名詞ではありませんが、4 つの単語で一つのまとまった意味を表し（「パンの焼き方」）、1 つの名詞と同じように使われます。このように、内部に S ＋ V を持たない数個の語群で、1 つの名詞と同じ働きをするものを「名詞句」と呼びます。

Today's lesson is on how to make bread.

How to make bread is not so difficult as you think. のような文もできます。

一方、（c）の下線部 that I will be a good cook は、内部に S ＋ V を持ち、全体として一つのまとまった意味を表して（「将来料理が上手になるだろうということ」）、1 つの名詞と同じように使われます。今回習ったように、このような節を「名詞節」と呼びます。

（例）

That I will be a good cook is certain.

It is certain that I will be a good cook.

（私が将来料理が上手になるということは確かだ）

Unit 11

形容詞節

ルール 1

1. （既習）英文には、[S＋V] の組合わせが 2 重・3 重に存在することがあります。こういう重層構造の文を「複文」と呼びます。

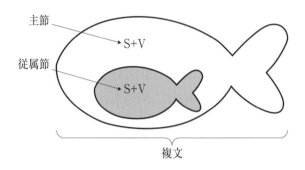

主節 ── S＋V

従属節 ── S＋V

複文

2. （既習）大きい方の [S＋V] から成る部分を「主節」、小さい方の [S＋V] から成る部分を「従属節」と呼びます。

3. 従属節で、一つの形容詞と同じように働くものを「形容詞節」と呼びます。

4. 形容詞節の特徴は：
   ◇その中に、小さな S と V を含む、
   ◇その直前にある名詞を修飾している、ことです。

5. 形容詞節は修飾語なので、文の骨組み（S＋V）ではありません。形容詞節をカッコに入れてしまうと、文の骨組みがよく見えてきます。

主節　　　　　　　　　　従属節

The man (who founded the Tokugawa Dynasty) is Tokugawa Ieyasu.

6. 代表的な形容詞節は、関係代名詞が作る節と、関係副詞が作る節です。
   次のような形をしています。詳しくは、Unit 12 で学習します。

関係代名詞が作る節
（節の中に S ＋ V を持つ）

This is the man (who founded the Tokugawa Dynasty).

直前に名詞　　関係代名詞

（語順訳）これがその人です（その人が徳川幕府を開きました）

（正式訳）これが、徳川幕府を開いた人です。

関係副詞が作る節
（節の中に S ＋ V を持つ）

This is the place (where Tokugawa Ieyasu was born).

直前に名詞　　関係副詞

（語順訳）ここがその場所です（その場所で徳川家康が生まれました）

（正式訳）ここが、徳川家康が生まれた場所です。

長文：The Tunnel of the Blue

Vocabulary Hints: 次の 1～13 の語の説明を、下の a～m から選んで補いなさい。

1. bank	（名）	2. isolate	（動）	3. except	（前）
4. path	（名）	5. steep	（形）	6. cliff	（名）
7. canyon	（名）	8. geography	（名）	9. chisel	（名）
10. pickaxe	（名）	11. across	（副）	12. follower	（名）
13. instead of					

説明

a. ～を除いては	b. 地形	c. ノミ（工具）	d. ツルハシ（工具）	e. 険しい
f. 細道	g. 信者	h. 峡谷	i. 断崖	j. ～の代わりに
k. 直径が	l. separate	m. the side of a river		

Part 1

1．樋田村の住民は、毎年数人が事故で亡くなっていました、それは何故でしたか？
2．禅海和尚はどのような旅をしていましたか？

The story (which I read yesterday) was very interesting. It is a true story about a traveling priest whose name was Zenkai. It was in the middle of Edo-period, and Zenkai was traveling around Oita Prefecture on his religious tour. One day he heard about a small village which was named Hida. The village stood on the bank of the Yamakuni River. The village was isolated from the nearby towns; there was no road that connected the village with other villages and towns, except a narrow path along the steep cliff of the canyon. Every year, several villagers slipped off the cliff, fell into the canyon, and got killed.

Part 2

Part 2 内容理解 🔊))

1．禅海和尚は村人を救うために、何を提案しましたか？
2．村人たちはなぜ禅海和尚の提案に耳を貸さなかったのですか？
3．村人に受け入れられなかった禅海和尚はどうしましたか？

Zenkai heard the story and felt very sorry for the villagers. He studied the geography of that area carefully. He found that the village and the nearest town were not far away. But there was a steep rocky mountain between the two, and it blocked the traffic.

"If we can dig a tunnel through the mountain," Zenkai thought, "it will solve the problem." He talked about his plan to the villagers. Nobody listened to this stranger who suddenly appeared in their village. Zenkai talked to the villagers again and again, but they only laughed and said, "It's impossible."

However, Zenkai did not give up. He started digging a hole into the mountain alone, with a chisel, a hammer, and a pickaxe. In his time, the only way to dig a tunnel was by hand. From morning till night, he kept digging all alone. One week passed, but the tunnel was only 50 centimeters deep. One month passed, but it was only 3 meters deep. The mountain that separated the village from the town was about 140 meters across. The villagers thought he was crazy. Nevertheless, Zenkai did not give up.

Part 3

Part 3 内容理解 🔊

1. 禅海和尚は何を食べ、どこで寝泊まりしていましたか？
2. 村人たちの、禅海和尚への態度は、どのように変化しましたか？
3. トンネルは、何年かけて貫通しましたか？
4. 菊池寛と禅海和尚とは、どのような関係ですか？

He ate the little food which some Buddhist followers gave him, slept in the tunnel, and went on digging. As several months passed, some villagers began to join him one by one. Slowly but steadily, the tunnel became longer and longer. Gradually, the villagers shared the same dream with Zenkai, to connect the village with the outer world with a tunnel. The villagers were united with a bright hope, and worked together.

It took 30 years for Zenkai and the villagers to complete the tunnel. Now the villagers were able to go to the town in 30 minutes through the tunnel, instead of along the dangerous path that used to take them more than three hours. The tunnel which was dug by Zenkai still remains in Yabakei, Oita. Later, a novelist named Kikuchi Kan wrote a novel based on Zenkai's story. It is 'Onshuno Kanatani'.

英問英答 🔊

Answer these questions in English.

(1) What was the name of the priest who was traveling in Kyushu?

(2) Why did Zenkai take interest in the small village named Hida?

(3) What separated Hida village from the nearest town?

(4) How big was the mountain that separated the village from the town?

(5) Why didn't the villagers listen to Zenkai's ideas at first?

(6) How long did it take for Zenkai and the villagers to complete the tunnel?

語順訳

次の文を語順訳しなさい。

(1) It is a true story/ about a traveling priest/ whose name was Zenkai.

(2) There was no road/ that connected the village with other villages and towns,/

except a narrow path/ along the steep cliff of the canyon.

(3) The mountain/ that separated the village from the town/ was about 140 meters

across.

(4) The tunnel/ which was dug by Zenkai/ still remains in Yabakei, Oita.

(5) A novelist named Kikuchi Kan/ wrote a novel/ based on Zenkai's story.

発見学習

　上の物語中の、形容詞節を（　　）で括りなさい。また、それがどの名詞を修飾しているかを、例にならって矢印で表しなさい。

例：The story (which I read yesterday) was very interesting.

形容詞ではないけれども、形容詞と同じ働きをする語句には、次のようなものがあります。

Look at the white cat.　形容詞

① Look at the sleeping cat.　現在分詞　（Unit 6B で学習）

② Look at the cat sleeping under the bed.　形容詞句（Unit 6B で学習）

③ Look at the cat which is sleeping under the bed.　関係代名詞が作る形容詞節

④ This is the village where I was born.　関係副詞が作る形容詞節

　上の③と④のように、関係代名詞（who, which, that）や関係副詞（where, when, how）が作る節のことを、関係詞節とも呼びます。これについては更に Unit 12 で学習します。

関係代名詞と関係副詞

Unit 11 で学んだように、形容詞節を作る主なものは、関係代名詞と関係副詞です。この Unit では、この2つを更に学習します。

発見学習

関係代名詞・関係副詞は、それを含んだ実際の英文に多く接して、そこからルールを見いだしていく方が、解りやすいです。

課題 1. 次の文の下線部に、語群から正しい語句を選んで補いなさい。

1.　The man that invented the electric light is ＿＿＿＿＿＿.

2.　The artist that painted Guernica is ＿＿＿＿＿＿.

3.　The samurai that built Kumamoto Castle is ＿＿＿＿＿＿.

4.　The composer that composed *Swan Lake* is ＿＿＿＿＿＿.

5.　The man that made the first complete map of Japan in the Edo peirod is ＿＿＿＿＿＿.

6.　The man that founded Waseda University is ＿＿＿＿＿＿.

7.　The explorer that first reached the South Pole is ＿＿＿＿＿＿.

8.　The month that comes between April and June is ＿＿＿＿＿＿.

9.　The high mountain that stands on the border of Shizuoka and Yamanashi Prefectures is ＿＿＿＿＿＿.

10.　The large lake that lies in Shiga Prefecture is ＿＿＿＿＿＿.

11.　The large shrine that stands in Ise, Mie Prefecture is ＿＿＿＿＿＿

12.　＿＿＿＿＿＿ is an animation film that Miyazaki Hayao made.

13.　＿＿＿＿＿＿ is a computer that Steve Jobs created.

14.　＿＿＿＿＿＿ is the food company that Colonel Sanders started in 1930.

15.　＿＿＿＿＿＿ is the castle that Tokugawa Ieyasu built in 1603.

16.　＿＿＿＿＿＿ is the picture that Pablo Picasso painted in 1937.

語群（アルファベット順）					
Amundsen	Edison	Guernica	Ino Tadataka	Ise Jingu	
Kato Kiyomasa	KFC	Lake Biwa	Laputa	May	Macintosh
Mt. Fuji	Nijojo	Ohkuma Shigenobu		Picasso	Tchaikovsky

課題2. 上の文章 1〜16 の中の、関係代名詞が作る従属節を（　　）でくくり、それが何を修飾しているかを矢印で示しなさい。

課題3. 従属節内には、必ず S と V が存在します。上の文章中の S に ◯ を付け、V に下線を引きなさい。

（例）My friend Mei's dream is to build a man-powered airplane (that can fly for more than two hours).

課題4. 上の文章では、従属節の中で関係代名詞が S になっているものと、O（目的語）になっているものに分かれます。その文章の番号を記入しなさい。

文章番号	
	関係代名詞が節の中の S になっている。
	関係代名詞が節の中の O になっている。

　節の中で O になっている関係代名詞は、省略されることがあります。例えば、

The book (which) I bought yesterday was very interesting. のように。

課題5. それでは、このテキストに出て来た関係代名詞と関係副詞を振り返ってみましょう。下記の①〜⑧の文について、

（ア）それぞれの文の関係代名詞が作る従属節を（　　）でくくり、それが何を修飾しているかを矢印で示しなさい。

（イ）その従属節内の S に ◯ を付け、V に下線を引きなさい。

（ウ）関係代名詞が省略できる文の番号を指摘しなさい。

（エ）関係副詞が作る従属節を（　　）でくくり、それが何を修飾しているかを矢印で示しなさい。

（Unit 5B）

① The Japanese man who had been shipwrecked and saved by the American ship drank something red that looked like human blood for the first time in his life.

（Unit 9）

② It is a website where you can find people all over the world looking for Email friends.

（Unit 11）

③ The story which I read yesterday was very interesting.

④ It is a true story about a traveling priest whose name was Zenkai.

⑤ One day he heard about a small village which was named Hida.

⑥ There was no road that connected the village with other villages and towns.

⑦ Nobody listened to this stranger who suddenly appeared in their village.

⑧ The mountain that separated the village from the town was about 140 meters across.

⑨ He ate the little food which some Buddhist followers gave him.

⑩ The tunnel which was dug by Zenkai still remains in Yabakei, Oita.

＊なお、関係代名詞 who と which は、常に that に代えることができます。

参考文：A Tribute to the Dog 🔊
by George G. Vest

　ここに紹介するのは、アメリカの若き弁護士 George G. Vest が 1855 年に担当した、犬殺害事件の裁判で述べた弁論です。その事件とは、ある土地の所有者が、そこに侵入してきた他人の飼い犬を銃で射殺したという事件でした。愛犬を殺された飼い主は、憤ってその所有者を訴えました。土地所有者は、自分の土地には 'Trespassers will be shot.'（侵入者は銃撃する。）という掲示を掲げてあり、それを無視して侵入した犬に落ち度があると主張しました。Vest は犬の飼い主だった友人に頼まれて原告側弁護人を担当し、最終陳述で次のように語りました。彼の陳述は陪審員たちの胸を深く打ち、裁判は原告の勝訴に終わりました。

　論述は 3 段落で構成されていますが、最初の 2 段落では関係代名詞による形容詞節が多く用いられ、それが人間の不誠実さと、犬の忠実さを聞き手の心に強く印象づける効果を発揮しています。一見難しく見えるかもしれませんが、この授業でやったように、形容詞節をカッコにくくってみると、けっこう分かりやすい文章だということが実感できると思います。（下記の文では、既にカッコでくくってあります。）

Gentlemen of the jury: The best friend (a man has in the world) may turn against him and become his enemy. His son or daughter (that he has reared with loving care) may prove ungrateful. Those (who are nearest and dearest to us), those (whom we trust with our happiness and our good name) may become traitors to their faith. The money (that a man has,) he may lose. It flies away from him, perhaps when he needs it most. A man's reputation may be sacrificed in a moment of ill-considered action. The people (who are prone to fall on their knees to do us honor when success is with us,) may be the first to throw the stone of malice when failure settles its cloud upon our heads.

The one absolutely unselfish friend (that man can have in this selfish world), the one (that never deserts him), the one (that never proves ungrateful or treacherous) is his dog. A man's dog stands by him in prosperity and in poverty, in health and in sickness. He will sleep on the cold ground, (where the wintry winds blow and the snow drives fiercely,) if only he may be near his master's side. He will kiss the hand (that has no food to offer); he will lick the wounds and sores (that come in encounter with the roughness of the world). He guards the sleep of his pauper master as if he were a prince. When all other friends desert, he remains. When riches take wings, and reputation falls to pieces, he is as constant in his love as the sun in its journey through the heavens.

If fortune drives the master forth, an outcast in the world, friendless and homeless, the faithful dog asks no higher privilege than that of accompanying him, to guard him against danger, to fight against his enemies. And when the last scene of all comes, and death takes his master in its embrace and his body is laid away in the cold ground, no matter if all other friends pursue their way, there by the graveside will the noble dog be found, his head between his paws, his eyes sad, but open in alert watchfulness, faithful and true even in death.

（出典：The History Place: Great Speeches Collection.　*https://www.historyplace.com/speeches/vest.htm*）

Unit 13

副詞節

ルール 1

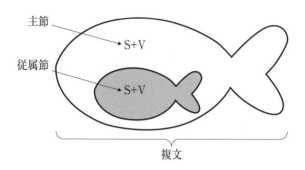

主節 → S+V

従属節 → S+V

複文

1. （既習）英文には、[S + V] の組合わせが 2 重・3 重に存在することがあります。これを「複文」と呼びます。

2. （既習）大きい方の [S + V] から成る部分を「主節」、小さい方の [S + V] から成る部分を「従属節」と呼びます。

3. 従属節で、一つの副詞と同じように働くものを「副詞節」と呼びます。

4. 副詞節には次のようなものがあります。副詞節は、始まりに接続詞がありますから、それを合図として見つけることができます。

> 「時」を表す副詞節：when〜，before〜，after〜等で始まる
> 「条件」を表す副詞節：if〜，even if〜等で始まる
> 「理由」を表す副詞節：because〜，since〜等で始まる
> 「譲歩」（〜だけれども）を表す副詞節：though〜，although〜等で始まる

発見学習 🔊

次の文は、イタリア旅行のアドバイスを述べたものです。各文中の副詞節を、例にならって（　　）で囲みなさい。

Example：（Before you go on a trip,） you should buy travel insurance.

（1） Insurance will help you when you get medical treatment in a foreign country.

（2） Even if some stranger offers you a free ride, you should not accept such an offer.

（3） You should not accept such an offer because you can be a victim of a crime.

（4） Though service in Italian restaurants, trains and offices may be slower than in Japan, people are not irritated with it.

長文：Traveling Tips in Japan and Italy

内容理解 ◀))

次の文は、日本とイタリアの旅行事情を比較したものです。その要点を表した表の空所①〜⑥に、下の英文中からキーワードを補いなさい。（何も言及していない項目には斜線を入れてあります。）

	日本	イタリア
ホテルの客室	ほとんどがバスタブあり	①
ホテルの食事		②
従業員へのチップの習慣	③	④
公衆トイレ	見つけやすい（駅・銀行・コンビニ・パチンコ店等）	⑤
公共の場での忘れ物	誰かがサービスカウンターに届けてくれることが多い	⑥

Part 1〜2 Vocabulary Hints: 次の 1〜14 の語の説明を、下の a〜n から選んで補いなさい。◀))

1. appear	（動）	2. soak	（動）	3. reservation	（名）
4. serve	（動）	5. beverage	（名）	6. tip	（動）
7. bellboy	（名）	8. expect	（動）	9. luggage	（名）
10. complain	（動）	11. uncivilized	（形）	12. customer	（名）
13. clerk	（名）	14. token	（名）		

説明

a. 客	b. 予約	c. 当然のこととして期待する	d. しるし
e. 〜のように見える	f. 〜に浸す	g. 不平を言う	h. drink
i. give some money to thank for some service		j. receptionist	k. give
l. a man who works in a hotel, carrying bags to the guests' rooms			m. very rude
n. suitcases, bags, etc that you have with you when traveling			

Part 1

Although the hotels in Japan and Italy may appear similar, there are several differences between them. Most hotels in Japan have a bathtub in the guest room. So you can take a bath freely whenever you like. Most hotels in Italy, on the other hand, have only a shower with no bathtub, except in high-class hotels. Therefore, if you really want to soak yourself in the bath in Italy, check if your hotel has a bathtub before making a reservation.

Most Italian hotels don't serve dinner. They only serve free breakfast. Some hotels serve very good food and a variety of beverages for breakfast, but others only serve bread and coffee. When you choose a hotel, check the menu of the breakfast on their web page.

Part 2

In Japanese hotels and restaurants, people do not have a custom of tipping the service staff. Even if the bellboy carries your suitcases from the entrance to your room, you don't have to give him a tip. But in Italian hotels, you are expected to give him a tip, for example a few Euros, after he has carried your luggage for you. The bellboy will not complain even if you don't give him any tip. But you will be considered an ill-mannered, uncivilized customer. When you ask the hotel clerks for some extra service – such as making an appointment at the doctor's office for you – you are also expected to give them a tip as a token of appreciation.

Part 3〜4 Vocabulary Hints: 次の 1〜8 の語の説明を、下の a〜h から選んで補いなさい。 🔊

1. neat	（形）	2. bar	（名）	3. final	（形）
4. attitude	（名）	5. lost article		6. deliver	（動）
7. precious	（形）	8. belonging	（名）		

説明

a. こぎれいな	b. 落とし物	c. 届ける	d. バール	e. 所持品
f. last	g. valuable	h. the way you think and feel about it		

Part 3

When you want to go to the public toilet in Japan, it is easy to find one. You will find neat and clean free toilets in stations, banks, convenience stores, pachinko halls, etc. In Italy, on the other hand, it is not easy to find public toilets quickly. There are not many convenience stores in Italy. Small stations do not have toilets. Even in big stations, it is not easy to find signs for toilets because the signs are small and different from Japan's. When you really need to go to the toilet as soon as possible, I recommend going into a bar. There are bars on almost every corner of towns in Italy. Go to the bar counter and ask for a glass of soda or a cup of coffee. Then ask the bartenders, "Posso usare il bagno, per favore?" (Can I use the toilet?) They will be happy to let you use their toilet.

Part 4

A final difference between the two countries is the attitude towards lost articles in public places such as on transportation and in the street. In Japan, even if you carelessly leave your camera or wallet behind in a public place, in most cases some kind person will deliver it to the service counter. This does not always happen in many other countries. Do not carelessly put your precious belonging on a bench or a seat in a public place. Look around when you are leaving your seat.

英問英答 🔊

Answer these questions in English.

(1) Do most guest rooms in Italy have bathtubs?

(2) What do we need to check when we choose a hotel in Italy?

(3) What will happen if a guest does not give a tip to the bellboy in Italy?

(4) Is it easy to find a public toilet in a town in Italy?

(5) Why is it sometimes difficult to find a toilet in big stations in Italy?

(6) What does the author recommend doing when we need to use the toilet in a hurry in Italy?

次の文を語順訳しなさい。

（1） Although/ the hotels in Japan and Italy/ may appear similar,/ there are several

differences/ between them.

（2） If you really want/ to soak yourself in the bath in Italy,/ check/ if your hotel

has a bathtub/ before making a reservation.

（3） In Italian hotels,/ you are expected to give him a tip,/ for example a few

Euros,/ after he has carried your luggage for you.

（4） When you ask the hotel clerks for some extra service/ – such as making an

appointment at the doctor's office for you/ – you are also expected to give them

a tip/ as a token of appreciation.

（5） Even if/ you carelessly leave your camera or wallet behind/ in a public place,/ in

most cases/ some kind person will deliver it/ to the service counter.

課題 1. 次の英文中の副詞節を発見し、（　　　）で括りなさい。

（1）Although the hotels in Japan and Italy may appear similar, there are several differences between them.

（2）So you can take a bath freely whenever you like.

（3）When you choose a hotel, check the menu of the breakfast on their web page.

（4）Even if the bellboy carries your suitcases from the entrance to your room, you don't have to give him a tip in Japan.

（5）Even in big stations, it is not easy to find signs for toilets because the signs are small and different from Japan's.

課題 2. 課題 1 で括った副詞節の意味を、次の 4 つに分類しなさい。

（ア）「時」when～，before～，after～

（イ）「条件」if～，even if～

（ウ）「理由」because～，since～

（エ）「譲歩」（～だけれども）though～，although～

課題 3. 上の (1)～(5) の英文の主節の S に下線を引き、V を○で囲みなさい。

ルール2

副詞的修飾語には、（ア）副詞、（イ）副詞句、（ウ）副詞節、があります。

（ア）副詞　　The ship will arrive tomorrow.

（イ）副詞句　The ship will arrive on Monday.

（ウ）副詞節　The ship will arrive after the storm is gone.

　　　　　　The ship will arrive when the clock strikes eleven.

Unit 14

過去完了形

ルール 1

動詞には［原形］［現在形］［過去形］［過去分詞形］があります。（Unit 1B, 5A, 7 で既習）

動詞の種類	原形	現在形	過去形	過去分詞形
be 動詞	be	am/is/are	was/were	been
一般動詞（規則変化）	walk	walk	walked	walked
一般動詞（不規則変化）	break	break	broke	broken

復習

動詞の過去分詞は、次のように用いられます。

（1）John has broken the glass.　［have/has＋過去分詞］で**現在完了形**

（2）John had broken the glass before I could stop him.

　　　　　　　　［had＋過去分詞］で**過去完了形**

（3）The glass was broken by John.　［be 動詞＋過去分詞］で**受動態**

（4）The glass broken by John was very expensive.　[**過去分詞の形容詞的用法**]

課題 1. 次の文中の過去分詞形に下線を引きなさい。

課題 2. それが

　　　　・受動態

　　　　・過去分詞の形容詞的用法

　　　　・現在完了形

のどの用法かを、「受」「形」「完」で答えなさい。

Unit 1A

受

（例） During World War II, London was <u>attacked</u> by German airplanes many times.

（1） Fortunately, nobody was injured, but the store building was damaged.

（2） The entrance of the store was blown off.

（3） But people were more surprised when they saw the familiar big sign 'OPEN' standing at the gate, and 'MORE' was added before the word 'OPEN'.

Unit 1B

（4） The story of Robinson Crusoe was based on a real person.

（5） Four years later, Alexander was rescued by the ship.

Unit 2A

（6） During her stay, she was very impressed with one thing.

Unit 4B

（7） Have you ever talked with foreign people?

Unit 5A

（8） Have you worked at a barbecue restaurant before, Junya?

（9） But I have eaten at your restaurant many times.

（10） I have been studying English for six and a half years.

（11） Have you washed your hands yet?

(12) It seems I have lost my wallet somewhere. I have no money with me.

Unit 6B

(13) Woodcutter, you have made me very happy with your honesty.

Unit 7

(14) Beef imported from America is cheaper than Japanese beef.

(15) A chartered bus was driving along the country road in Maizuru-shi, Kyoto-fu.

(16) On that day, Western Japan was hit by a very big typhoon.

(17) Because of the flood, the traffic was paralyzed on the road.

(18) People's feet and knees were covered with the flood waters.

(19) They were enormously encouraged by the singing.

(20) The bus was discovered by an SDF helicopter.

(21) One by one, the people were lifted up into the helicopter.

(22) This story was published in a book entitled 'Bus Suibotsu Jiko.'

Unit 9

(23) Have you ever used English for a real purpose?

(24) According to recent studies, language is best acquired through understanding plenty of meaningful language input.

Unit 11

(25) The tunnel which was dug by Zenkai still remains in Yabakei, Oita.

(26) Later, a novelist named Kikuchi Kan wrote a novel based on Zenkai's story.

Unit 13

(27) But in Italian hotels, you are expected to give him a tip, for example a few Euros, after he has carried your luggage for you.

(28) A final difference between the two countries is the attitude towards lost articles in public places such as on transportation and in the street.

課題 3. 上で下線を引いた過去分詞のうちから、不規則変化をする動詞を抜き出し、その活用を書きなさい。

現在形	過去形	過去分詞形

ルール 2

　過去完了形［had＋過去分詞］は、

　・同一文中またはその前後の文中に、2つの過去の出来事（状態）が登場して、

　・その一方の出来事や状態が他方より古い場合に、

　・古い方を過去完了形にする、

という使い方をします。

（例） When $\boxed{\text{I arrived at the station}}$, $\boxed{\text{the train had already left}}$.

　　　　　　　　新しい過去　　　　　　　　　　古い過去

【練習】

　次の文の中には、2つの過去の出来事が描かれています。より古い方の出来事を過去完了形にしなさい。

（1）　Yesterday I carelessly <u>broke</u> the lamp that I <u>bought</u> in Spain 20 years ago.
　　　　（昨日私はうっかりして、20年前にスペインで買ったランプを壊してしまった）

（2）　I <u>could recognize</u> the man easily because I <u>saw</u> him on TV many times.
　　　　（私はその男を TV で何度も見たことがあったので、すぐに彼だとわかった）

（3）　The boy <u>said</u> that he <u>was</u> sick for three days.
　　　　（少年は、3日間具合が悪かったと言った）

（4）　Hilary and Temjin <u>climbed</u> up the mountain which nobody <u>climbed</u> before.
　　　　（ヒラリーとテムジンは、それまで誰も登ったことのなかった山に登った）

伝わりやすい英文を作る秘訣

　筆者はこれまで、大勢の学習者の英文を添削してきました。中には、そんなに英語力レベルは高くないけれども、自分の力で扱い得る英文を上手に積み上げて、わかりやすい上等の英文を作る人がいました。一方では、自分の手に負えないような複雑な文構造で、強引に英語に直し、ほとんど意味を成していない英文もありました。言葉は、相手に理解されてはじめて意味を持つものですから、理解してもらえるように書くことが、何よりも大切です。この課では、背伸びすることなく、シンプルだがすっきりと意味の通る、英語らしい英文を作る秘訣を紹介します。

ルール

1. 最初から英語で発想しよう

　日本語で原稿を書いてから英訳しようとすると、不自然な英文となります。なぜなら、日本語の語順と英語の語順が大きく異なるからです。

　たとえば、「私がこの大学を選んだ理由は、L大学と交流があるからです。」という日本語原稿を作って、それを英訳しようとすると、

× The reason why I chose this university is that it has exchange with L University.
　といった英文になりがちです。これは不必要に複雑で、ぎこちない文です。

　上の文は、"I chose this university because it has exchange with L University." とすれば、もっと平易で自然な英文となります。
　本書では、このような自然な英文を作るためのもっと良い作文法を2つ紹介します。

良い作文法1.　最初から英語で発想する

　最初から英語で発想するためには、ブレーンマップを描いて、アイディアを図示することから始めましょう。
　図1は、Unit 9の長文 What Is the Best Way to Learn English? を書く準備として描いたブレーンマップです。用紙の中心に自分のテーマを大きなバルーンに書き、それについて考えつくことを周囲の小さなバルーンに書き、そこから派生する事柄を更に破線のバルーンで付け足しています。

ここまで準備しておけば、あとはこれらのバルーン同士を表わしやすいＳ（主語）とＶ（述語動詞）で組んでみれば、素直な英語になります。

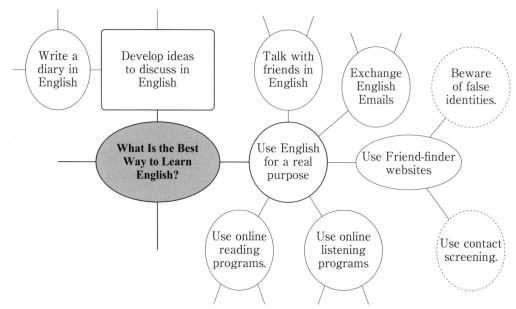

図1：'What Is the Best Way to Learn English?' を書く準備としての brain map の一例

良い作文法 2.　最初から英語が無理なら、英語用の日本語で発想しよう

やむなく日本語で発想する場合は、日本語原稿→英語用日本語原稿→英語原稿の手順をとることです。ここでも、何を主語とし、何を述語動詞とするかが、最も重要です。

（例）「そんなにタバコを吸うと、健康の害になりますよ。」を英訳してみましょう。

→　日本語では省かれているが英語では必要な部分を補い、英語の語順に入れ替え、英訳用の日本語原稿を作ります。

→「もしも / あなたが / 吸うならば / そんなに / 多くの / タバコを、/ あなたは / 害することでしょう / あなたの健康を。」

→これを、英語に変えます。

→ **If you smoke so many cigarettes, you will ruin your health.**

こうして、素直で英語らしい英訳になりました。

2. 英語は「何を主語にするか」で、文の質が決まる

以前、筆者が親善通訳として、代々木オリンピック記念ユースホステルで開かれた国際青年交流イベントで、ある国からの青年代表団を迎えた時のこと。その国は権威主義的な国で、団長は国立大学の年配の教授、ことごとく、一般団員とは違う特別待遇を要求する人でした。

ユースホステルですから、自分のベッドには自分でシーツや枕カバーを付けなければなりません。「困ったな、そんなことは召使いがやることだ、とゴネるだろうな」と心配しながら、私は

彼の部屋を訪ねました。案の定、彼はシーツや枕カバーを受け取ったまま放置しています。いろいろ表現を選択した上で、私はこう切り出しました。

"Professor, in youth hostels, we make our own bed. Here is your sheet and pillow case. Would you like me to show you how to do that?"

すると教授は、以外と素直に私の言葉を受け止め、「自分でやるからいい」と答えたのです。その時私は、"We make our own bed." という表現の効果を実感しました。実はさっきまで私は、"Please make your own bed." という文型で話そうとしていたのですが、とっさに浮かんできた "We make" に代えたのです。それが彼の態度を軟化させたと思われるのです。

Please make your own bed. という言い方は、Please は付いているものの、文体は命令文なので、言われた方はドキッとします。

また、You must make your own bed. という言い方をしても、you must はダイレクトに相手を指して強制する表現です。

それに対して、We make our own bed. は、「そういうしきたりです」という事実のみを伝え、決断を相手に委ねています。しかも主語が we なので、「あなたも私も仲間です」という friendly な立場に立っています。

英語では、同じ事を言うにも、主語の選び方で幾通りもの言い方が可能です。その複数の選択肢の中から、

①どの主語を選んだら、より平易で英語らしい文ができるか、

②どの主語を選んだら、文の堅さ（学術的 or 日常的か、理知 or 情緒か）、親しみやすさ（権威的 or フレンドリーか）、対人的距離（間接的か直接的か）を適切に調節できるかを考えて、文を作りましょう。

たとえば「艱難汝を玉にす」ということわざを英訳する場合を考えてみましょう。「苦難や災難があなたという人間を宝石のように磨いてくれる」という意味です。主語の選び方で、次のように色々な文章ができます。

① You will be able to improve yourself by overcoming a hardship.

② People grow up through overcoming difficulties.

③ Difficulty is the nurse of greatness.

④ Adversity makes people wise.

①の文は、代名詞 you を主語にしているため、パーソナルで日常的な親しみやすさを持っています。②は、「人々」という日常語を主語にしているため、客観的ではあるが日常的な雰囲気です。③の文は、「困難」という抽象名詞を主語にしているため、やや堅い雰囲気です。④は 'adversity'（逆境）という、非日常的な抽象名詞を主語にしており、［SVC］よりもパワーの強い［SVO］の文型でできているので、非常に堅く権威的な雰囲気になっています。

3. 「主語＋述語動詞」の組み合わせを少なくしよう

　時々、「長々と続く複雑で難解な英文が、高級な英文だ」と信じている英語学習者に出会います。これはとんでもない誤解です。同じ事柄を伝えるのに、一番シンプルで短い文こそが、高級な英文なのです。1つの文中の「S＋V」の組み合わせは、少ないほど好ましいのです。複複文（同一文中に［S＋V］の組合せが3重になっているもの）などは、避けたい文体です。同じ事を言うのに、できるだけ平易な文体を使う、それが上手なライターです。次の2つの例でそれを実感してください。

（例）彼が、自分でやると言ったことを実行しなかったことは残念なことだ。

a）◎ Unfortunately, he did not keep his promise.

b）× It is a regret that he did not do what he had said he would do.

練習1

　次の英訳は、不必要に複雑です。S＋V の組み合わせを少なくして、改良してみよう。

---

(1) このことわざがわたしのモットーであるのは、私がこのことわざに救われた経験があるからです。

× The reason why this saying is my motto is that I have an experience in which I was saved by this saying.

(2) 彼女の考えとは、バイオリンを通じて、音楽が楽しいことを子供たちに感じさせることでした。

× Her mind was that she made children feel that music was fun through the violin.

(3) 筆者が留学にメリットがないと考えた理由は、彼女が期待していたほど効果が得られなかったからだろう。

× The reason why the writer thought that there was no advantage of studying abroad may be that there seems not so much effect than she had expected.

3-1.　［S＋V］の組み合わせを少なくする方法

［S＋V］の組み合わせを少なくするには、次の方法が効果的です。

a）長い文は 2〜3 文に分割する。

上の練習 1 を例にとると：

"Once this saying saved me. That is why it has become my motto." のように、2 文にすれば、楽に表現できます。

b）前置詞 with を活用する

With は、「〜を持っている」という意味を表わし、文の簡略化に有効です。

△ The house whose roof is red is our school.

◎ The house with a red roof is our school.

○ I like people who have strong individuality.

◎ I like people with strong individuality.

c）節ではなく語句を使う。

He did not do what he had promised.（節）

He did not keep his promise.（語句）

It is a regret that she has failed.（節）

Unfortunately, she has failed.（語句）

4.　日本語の［〜は］にまどわされないように

日本語の格助詞「〜は」は、必ずしも主語を表すものではありません。たとえば「犬は嫌いだ」では、「犬を嫌いだ」を意味しています。ですから、「〜は」の部分を自動的に英語の主部にしてしまってはいけません。日本語では「僕はカレーだ」と言っても通じます。しかし英語で "I am curry." とはできません。なぜならば、"I" は人間、"curry" は物、人間がカレーに変身するわけがないからです。英語では、［人間＝物］のように同列視した文構造は非論理的で不可とされます。

練習 2

次の［主語＋述語動詞］はどこがおかしいでしょうか？

（1）Tokyo is a lot of people.（東京には多くの人がいる）

（2）Lake Yamanaka is many fish.（山中湖には多くの魚がいる）

（3）The Japanese room is tatami-mat.（日本式の部屋は畳の部屋だ）

（4）Youth hostels can stay four to eight guests in a room.（ユースホステルでは一室に 4〜8 人が泊まれます）

5. "旧情報→ 新情報." の流れで

次の例を見てください。

There was once <u>a lazy boy named Bill</u>. One day <u>he</u> skipped school and went to <u>the movie</u>

<u>theater</u>. In <u>the theater</u>, he came across his cram school teacher, <u>Ms. Brown</u>. <u>Ms.Brown</u> was watching

Star Wars II with <u>a handsome young man</u>. "<u>That man</u> must be her boyfriend," Bill thought.

この文は、

〈パターン 1〉情報 A　　+　　情報 B

　　　　　　　情報 B　　+　　情報 C

　　　　　　　　　　　情報 C　　+　　情報 D

　　　　　　　　　　　　　　情報 D　　+　　情報 E

というふうに、前の文の最後に登場した人や物を、次の文の主部に受け継ぐ文体をしています。こうすることによって、「今、何を話題にしているか」を読み手に分かりやすくしています。

〈パターン 2〉もう一つのパターンを見てみましょう。

Jim was born in London in 1960.

He entered Oxford University in 1980.

He met his future wife Linda in 1981.

He got a job at the British Railways soon after graduation.

情報 A	+	情報 B
情報 A	+	情報 C
情報 A	+	情報 D
情報 A	+	情報 E

こちらの文体は、各文の主部を 1 つに固定して、述部に新情報を登場させています。それによってやはり、「今、何を話題にしているか」を読み手に分かりやすくしています。

6. パラレリズムを意識して

パラレリズム（対句表現）を使って、読者の文構造分析の負担を軽減することができます。下記の例文で、□で囲った語句は、それぞれが同じ形態で揃えてあるため、読み手の理解の負担を軽減します。文を作る時は、パラレリズムを利用するようにしましょう。

（例）

（1）This book is $\boxed{\text{useful}}$ but $\boxed{\text{boring}}$. （2つとも形容詞で揃えている）

（2）Mary is $\boxed{\text{tall}}$, $\boxed{\text{slender}}$, and $\boxed{\text{pretty}}$. （3つとも形容詞で揃えている）

（3）My grandma always tells me $\boxed{\text{to study hard}}$, $\boxed{\text{to come home early}}$, and $\boxed{\text{to eat a balanced diet}}$.
（3つとも不定詞の名詞的用法で揃えている）

（4）The man told me $\boxed{\text{why he left Russia}}$, $\boxed{\text{why he came to Australia}}$, and $\boxed{\text{why he wanted to}}$
$\boxed{\text{join the army}}$. （3つとも［疑問詞＋S＋V］で揃えている）

練習3

次の文のパラレリズムを整えて、もっと読みやすい文にしよう。

（1）To err is human, but forgiving is divine. （過ちを犯すことはだれにでもある人間らしい性質だ、しかし、人の過ちを許すのは、神にも似た偉大な性質だ）

（2）It is very easy to start a war, but you cannot finish the war easily. （戦争を始めるのはいともたやすいが、それを終わらせるのは難しい）

（3）Praise others, and they will bring you happiness. If you curse others, they will bring you hatred. （人を誉めよ、そうすれば人はあなたに幸福をもたらす。もし人を呪えば、人はあなたに憎しみをもたらす）

（4）This proverb teaches us that children should not be spoiled but to make them experience hardship. （このことわざは、子供は甘やかすのでなく、困難を経験させるべきだということを我々に教えてくれる）

コミュニケーション活動集

言語の文法や表現は、ルールを学ぶだけでは不十分です。実際に2人あるいはそれ以上で、それを使いながら身につけてゆくことが効果的です。そのために、各ユニットの学習事項と関連のあるコミュニケーション活動を用意しました。習ったことを実際に使って自分を表現し、相互理解を深めてください。

　なお、話す時に人間は、「話す内容」と「文法的正確さ」を同時には考えられないことが証明されています。ですから話す際には、文法的正確さをあまり気にしないで、内容優先で話すことをおすすめします。

　書く時にも同様で、「文を生み出す」ことと「生み出した文の文法を整える」ことを、同時にはできないと言われています。ですから、英文を書く際には、まず正確さをあまり気にせずに、どんどん文を作り出すことを先に行い、それが済んでから、書いた文の正確さを整えることをおすすめします。

Unit 1A　主部と述語動詞 🔊
Communication: Talking About Your School Life

1.　SとVを上手に選んで、自己紹介の文章を作りましょう。下の例を参考に、5文以上の自己紹介を作りましょう。
2.　作った自己紹介を、ペアやグループで相手に伝えましょう。
3.　自己紹介を聞いた人は、次の人に、聞いた内容を他己紹介しよう。

Examples

	S（主部）	V（述語動詞）	
1	I	am	a student at Jonan College.
2	I	major	in biology at college.
3	My college	is	in the suburbs of Nagoya-shi.
4	I	commute	to school by train and bus.
5	It	takes	about seventy minutes.
6	I	enjoy	making new friends at college.
7	I	like	my psychology classes very much.
8	My dream	is	to become a clinical therapist.
9	My favorite pastime	is	singing songs in karaoke.

Unit 1B be 動詞と一般動詞 🔊
Communication: Calling Card Exchange

1. （授業前の準備） 右のような名刺を作り、6枚
   コピーして次の授業に持参します。
2. （授業中） 席を立って歩き、これまで話したこ
   とのない人を見つけて、名刺を渡し、英語で説明
   します。
3. （インタビュー後） もらった名刺をレポート用
   紙に貼り、名刺交換した感想を英文で書いて提出
   します。

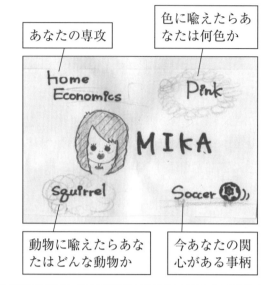

あなたの専攻

色に喩えたらあなたは何色か

動物に喩えたらあなたはどんな動物か

今あなたの関心がある事柄

─〈Example〉─────────────────────────────

Hello! Nice to meet you. My name is Mika. My major is home economics. My color is pink because I am always cheerful. My animal is squirrel because I move around quickly. I am interested in soccer. I like Jubiro Iwata.

─────────────────────────────────────

Unit 2A 肯定文・否定文・疑問文 🔊
Communication: Interviewing

　　先生があなたに、次の番号（①〜㉛）のどれかの文を割り当てます。その番号の文に書かれたことに該当する人を、教室を回って尋ね、探してみましょう。5分間でできるだけ多くの人と会話しましょう。下記の会話例を参考にしてください。

─〈Example〉─────────────────────────────

あなた：<u>Excuse me.</u> Do you want to live in a foreign country in the future?

A さん：No, I don't.

あなた：I see. Thank you. What is your question?

A さん：Do you like cats a lot?

あなた：Yes, I love cats.

A さん：Thank you. <u>Nice talking with you.</u>

─────────────────────────────────────

あなた：<u>Nice talking with you, too.</u>

　上記の下線部は、始めと終わりの挨拶として励行しましょう。

The List of Questions

① I want to live in a foreign country in the future.

② I love cats.

③ I like studying English.

④ I usually get up earlier than six o'clock.

⑤ I like cooking.

⑥ I like fishing.

⑦ I can catch a grasshopper in my hand.

⑧ I can swim more than 1000 meters.

⑨ I play some musical instrument, such as the piano, guitar, and clarinet.

⑩ I have been to Disneyland more than five times.

⑪ I have climbed Mt. Fuji.

⑫ I like jogging.

⑬ I believe in the existence of UFOs.

⑭ I like my school very much.

⑮ I have a part-time job.

⑯ I don't like watching TV.

⑰ I want to live longer than 90 years.

⑱ I sleep more than eight hours a day.

⑲ I can speak to girls easily.

⑳ I can speak to boys easily.

㉑ I keep a diary.

㉒ I go to the movies more than twice a month.

㉓ I am afraid of dogs.

㉔ I speak three or more languages.

㉕ I cook my own lunch.

㉖ I remember my father's birthday.

㉗ I have been to several foreign countries.

㉘ I soon get carsick.

㉙ I dance Yosakoi Dance.

㉚ I have picked up a large amount of money on the street.

㉛ I am good at singing karaoke.

Unit 2B 未来表現 🔊

Communication: Imagining Your Future

今から４年後のあなたはどういう風に暮らしているだろうか？ 例にならって、あなたの４年後の未来予想を描いてみよう。

〈Example〉

(a) What will you do after finishing college?

I will get a job./ I will go to a graduate school./ I will work abroad on working holiday./ I will take over my family job.

(b) Where will you live?

I will live in my home town. / I will live in a big city. / I will live in the countryside. /I will live in a foreign country.

(c) When will you get married?

I will get married at the age of 25. / I will get married after I am 30 years old. / I will never get married.

(d) How many children will you have?

I will have _____ children.

(e) What will you be doing to refresh yourself on holidays?

I will be practicing Yoga.

パートナーと、次の質問を尋ねあおう。

① What will you do after finishing college?

② Where will you live when you graduate from college?

③ When will you get married?

④ How many children will you have?

⑤ What will you be doing to refresh yourself?

Unit 3 助動詞 🔊

Communication: How Unique Are You?

Every one of you is a unique person. Your uniqueness is very precious. When you go abroad, people will want to know how unique you are.

What unique things can you do? Think and answer this question. Give three points that are unique to you.

Very small things are quite okay.

Sample Conversation

Ryo : <u>Hi, Yuka, How unique are you?</u>

Yuka : I can snap my fingers.

Ryo : Really. Can you show me?

Yuka : （snapping sound）

Ryo : That's wonderful!

Yuka : <u>How unique are you</u>, Ryo?

Ryo : I can turn a pencil on my fingers.

Yuka : Really. Can you show me?

Ryo : Sure. Like this.

Yuka : Wow, that's great!

Useful words	
cook Mexican food	make people laugh
move my ears	make funny faces
mimic Mikawa Kenichi	dance Hawaiian
sing rap music	speak Chinese
play tricks	juggle
draw a cartoon	play the clarinet
speak Portuguese	swim in four styles

Unit 4A　目的語・補語 🔊

Communication: Let's be Original and Unique!

Japanese society values harmony more than uniqueness. In Japan, you are safe as long as you think and act like other people.

However, this is not always true in many other countries. People value your own uniqueness and originality. They are not very interested in mere imitators without individuality.

Therefore, you should discover and treasure your own originality and uniqueness.

次の例にならって、ペアでお互いのユニークな点や、独自な点について話し合おう。

〈Example〉

A : What makes you unique?

B : I am a good cook. I cook Japanese, Chinese, Korean and Italian food.

A : Really! That's amazing.

B : Thank you. What makes you unique?

A : I am good at taking care of animals. I like cats, dogs, rabbits, hamsters, and even reptiles.

B : That's great! Do you want to be a zoo keeper?

A : Yes, that is my dream. How about you, C? What makes you unique?

C : I write and sing my own songs. I have more than a dozen original songs.

A and B : Wow! You are really original. We want to hear your songs.

Unit 5A　過去形と現在完了形 🔊
Communication: Have you ever ---?

現在完了形を使って、"Have you ever ---?"（あなたはこれまでに――をしたことがありますか？）の質問を作って来て下さい。次の授業で、その質問を 8 人の級友に尋ねて回る、インタビュー活動を行います。同時にあなたはその 8 人の級友たちから、質問を受けますから、それにも英語で答えましょう。下記はその会話例です。

〈Example〉

A : Excuse me. Have you ever seen a famous person?

B : Yes, I saw the Sumo Grand Champion Hakuhou on the Shinkansen train last year.

A : Oh, that's exciting. Now, what's your question?

B : Have you ever written a love letter?

A : No, I haven't. But I have received some love letters.

B : Really!! Good for you! Nice talking with you.

A : It was really nice talking with you.

Communication: My Favorite Place

All people have their favorite places somewhere. Some people love tourist places such as Kyoto and Nara. Some love scenic places like Kamikochi and Mt. Aso. Others like fun places such as Disneyland and Nagashima Amusement Park. Still others like places which have a special meaning for them. Follow the example below and talk about your favorite places in Japan, other than your own home.

〈Example〉

Lisa : What is your favorite place in Japan?

Ken : It is Tsugaike Highland Ski Resort in Nagano Prefecture.

Lisa : Why do you like the place?

Ken : Because it has excellent ski slopes. It also has a nice village with fancy hotels and restaurants. How about you? What is your favorite place in Japan?

Lisa : My favorite place is the seashore near my home town in Toyohashi. It's not at all famous, and usually there are no people. But you can see the wide Pacific Ocean and feel a pleasant sea breeze.

Ken : I see. I want to go to the beach, too.

Communication: Plans for the Summer Vacation

Summer vacation is coming. Some of you may be going back to your home town. Some of you may be planning to go on a sightseeing trip. And some of you may have a part-time job. Some of you may just stay home and relax. Let's have a conversation about the summer vacation.

〈Example〉

A : Do you have any plans for the summer vacation?

B : I am planning to go back to my home town in Matsue.

A : Oh, really. What are you planning to do there?

B : I am planning to meet my family. Also I am planning to meet my old friends from high school.

A : That will be exciting.

B : Yes, thank you. How about you?

A : I haven't made any plans yet. But I want to go somewhere on my bike.

B : That's a great idea. You like cycling?

A : I love cycling. I'm a member of the Cycling Club.

B : Great. Have a good time.

A : Thank you. You, too.

Unit 7 受動態と過去分詞 🔊
Communication: Famous Festivals – Where and When?

　日本や世界の面白いお祭りについて、ペアかグループで紹介し合いましょう。参考までに、下の表に8つの面白いお祭りの概要を載せました。次の会話例にならって、自分が調べてきたお祭りについてクイズ形式でメンバーに紹介し合いましょう。

〈Example〉

Members : Okay. Give us a hint.

Erika : 　This festival is very unique.

Members : Where is it held?

Erika : 　It is held in Spain.

Members : When is it held?

Erika : 　In late August.

Members : Is it Bull-fighting?

Erika : 　No, it's not. But you are partly right. People fight with each other in this festival.

Members : How do they fight? Do they punch or kick?

Erika : 　No, they don't. They throw something.

Members : I've heard about it. It's the Tomato Throwing Festival.

Erika : 　You're right. Good job.

Name of the festival	Features of the festival	Where it is held	When it is held
1. La Tomatina	Around 20,000 people throw over-ripe tomatoes at each other on the streets of a small town. More than 100 tons of tomatoes are thrown in this food fight. Anyone can participate in the tomato throwing if they win a ticket in the lottery.	Buñol, Valencia, Spain	4 days in late August
2. International Hot Air Balloon Festival	Hundreds of hot air balloons lift off one after another and sail through the sky. Visitors can get on one of the balloons if they wish.	Albuquerque, New Mexico, U.S.A	the first week in October
3. Inti Raymi	A big theatrical performance of Inca's religious celebration of the Sun God. Many of the leading actors and actresses in South America perform in traditional costumes around the historical remains of the Inca Empire.	Cusco, Peru	on the day of the winter solstice (late in June)
4. Carnival of Rio de Janeiro	Over 20 samba schools, i.e. groups, perform dancing and samba music with floats and colorful costumes. Each samba school has about 4000 dancers.	Rio de Janeiro, Brazil	4 days from the end of February to early March
5. Sapporo Snow Festival	Over 200 snow sculptures, some measuring more than 25 meters wide and 15 meters high, are exhibited here and there in the 1.5 kilometers long Odori Park. There are concerts, events, and a variety of food stalls around the park, too.	Sapporo, Hokkaido	early February for 12 days
6. Aoi Festival	Over 500 people are dressed in the aristocratic style of the Heian Period and walk down the main street. There are men on horseback, giant bouquets of flowers, decorated ox-drawn carts, and a large procession of women in kimono.	Kyoto city, Kyoto fu	May 15
7. Aomori Nebuta Festival	Nebutas are massive lantern floats 5 meters high, 9 meters wide, and 7 meters deep. Each nebuta represents well-known heroes/heroines based on kabuki or mythical stories. Each nebuta is accompanied by 500 to 2,000 Haneto, that is, dancers. The festival attracts around 3 million visitors from Japan and abroad.	Aomori city, Aomori ken	August 2 to 7
8. Naked Festival	A 1,200 year old ritual to dispel evil spirits and diseases and welcome in the good fortune. Thousands of naked men, only wearing white cotton loincloths, struggle to touch the Lucky Man as he makes his way to the inner shrine.	Konomiya, Inazawa, Aichi	early February

Unit 8 不定詞 🔊
Communication: What I Do for that Purpose

What do you do for the following purposes? First, fill in your own information. Next, walk around the classroom, find a partner, and exchange your answers.

Sheet A

To keep healthy, I _____.

To relax, I _____.

To get some pocket money, I _____.

Sheet B

To sleep well at night, I _____.

To cheer myself up, I _____.

To be a better person, I _____.

Unit 9 動名詞 🔊
The Right Person for the Right Job（適材適所）

1. 次の表の横軸 (a)〜(i) は、職業を表しています。(i) には、あなたが関心のある職業を追加してください。右端の (j) はあなた自身についての欄です。

2. 表の縦軸 1〜17 は、その職業に向いているかどうかの質問です。質問 17 には、あなたが必要だと思う質問を書き加えてください。

3. (j) の縦列で、あなた自身が当てはまるマスに ✔ を入れてみましょう。

4. あなた自身について答え終わったら、あなたの ✔ パターンと類似した ✔ パターンの職業があるかどうか、表の中でさがしてみよう。

		(a) tour guide	(b) counsellor	(c) translator	(d) police officer	(e) car mechanic	(f) fire fighter
1	Do you like working indoors? Yes		✔	✔			
2	Do you like working outdoors? Yes	✔			✔		✔
3	Do you like working alone? Yes	✔	✔	✔			
4	Do you like working in a team? Yes				✔		✔
5	Do you like meeting many people? Yes	✔	✔		✔		
6	Do you like working with your hands? Yes					✔	✔
7	Do you like working at a desk? Yes		✔	✔			
8	Do you like reading and writing? Yes			✔			
9	Do you enjoy taking care of animals? Yes				✔		
10	Do you enjoy doing judo or kendo? Yes				✔		
11	Do you enjoy working on machines? Yes					✔	✔
12	Are you interested in helping people? Yes	✔	✔		✔	✔	✔
13	Are you good at making people relax? Yes	✔	✔		✔		
14	Do you mind facing a dangerous situation? No				✔		✔
15	Do you mind traveling a lot? No	✔					
16	Do you mind getting dirty or muddy? No					✔	✔
17	Free question						

		(g) truck driver	(h) zoo keeper	(i)	(j) Yourself
1	Do you like working indoors? Yes				
2	Do you like working outdoors? Yes	✔	✔		
3	Do you like working alone? Yes	✔			
4	Do you like working in a team? Yes		✔		
5	Do you like meeting many people? Yes				
6	Do you like working with your hands? Yes		✔		
7	Do you like working at a desk? Yes				
8	Do you like reading and writing? Yes				
9	Do you enjoy taking care of animals? Yes		✔		
10	Do you enjoy doing judo or kendo? Yes				
11	Do you enjoy working on machines? Yes	✔			
12	Are you interested in helping people? Yes				
13	Are you good at making people relax? Yes				
14	Do you mind facing a dangerous situation? No		✔		
15	Do you mind traveling a lot? No	✔			
16	Do you mind getting dirty or muddy? No	✔	✔		
17	Free question				

＊この表に記入されたチェックは、1つの見解を表したもので、正式な調査にもとづくものではありません。

5. ペアやグループで、次のように対話してみよう。

〈Example〉

A : I like working outdoors. I like working on machines. And I don't mind getting dirty or muddy. Therefore, I think I would be a good car mechanic. Do you agree?

B : I do./ I'm not sure./ No, I don't.

A : I see. How about you?

B : I am good at making people relax. I like meeting many people. And I enjoy taking care of people. So I think I would be a good tour guide. Do you agree?

A : I do./ I'm not sure./ No, I don't.

Unit 10　名詞節 🔊
Communication: Do You Believe This?

　一般に通説とされている男性観、女性観を、あなたはどう思いますか？例にならって、意見を交換しよう。

〈Example〉

A : People say that men are usually brave. What do you think about it?

B : I don't think so. For example, I am a man but I'm not brave.

A : So, you don't think that men are usually brave.

B : That's right. People say that women are good at cooking. What do you think about it?

A : I think so. Most of my women friends can cook. But most of my men friends don't cook.

B : I see. Thank you.

　たとえばこんな通説をあなたはどう思いますか？次の通説の中から３つを選び、それについて友達の見解を尋ねてみましょう。

　What do you think about these common sayings?

1.　Men are usually brave.

2.　Men are usually strong-minded.

3.　Men are usually good at math and science.

4.　Men are usually good with mechanics.

5.　Men usually enjoy martial arts.

6. Men usually like going out better than staying home.

7. When a couple eats in a restaurant, the man should pay for all the food.

8. Women are usually good at cooking.

9. Women are usually tidy.

10. Women are usually tender-hearted.

11. Women are usually thrifty.

12. Women are usually talkative.

13. Women are usually good at housework.

Unit 11　形容詞節 🔊
Communication: I Like Those People Who

"What types of people do you like?" Have you ever asked this question to yourself? We all have three types of people around us; those people who we do not like, those who are all right to us, and those who we like and treasure. Too often, we care so much about the first category of people, and do not care enough for the third category of people. In this activity, you have a chance to ask yourself about your favorite types of people. Follow the example below and talk with your partners.

⟨Example⟩

Ken : What types of people do you like, Lisa?

Lisa : I like those people who are considerate to other people.

Ken : I see.

Lisa : What types of people do you like, Ken?

Ken : I like those people who keep their promises.

Lisa : Uhm hmm. I like that type of people, too.

Unit 12　関係代名詞と関係副詞 🔊
Communication: Which Foreign Country Do You Want to Visit?

Which foreign country do you want to visit in the future? What do you want to do there? Follow the example below and talk with your partner.

〈**Example**〉

Ken : Which foreign country do you want to visit in the future?

Lisa : I want to visit Cambodia.

Ken : Really. What do you want to do there?

Lisa : I want to visit Angkor Wat, the famous ruins of temples. I want to paint sketches of the temples.

Ken : Sounds fantastic.

Lisa : It really is. Which foreign country do you want to visit in the future, Ken?

Ken : I want to visit Brazil.

Lisa : Uhm humm. What do you want to do there?

Ken : I am really interested in the Amazon River. I like wild plants and animals. I want to walk in the tropical rain forest along the Amazon.

Lisa : Sounds exciting!

Unit 13   副詞節 🔊

Communication: What Do You Do in Such Occasions?

こんな時、あなたはどうしますか？例の下線部に続けて、自分を表現してみましょう。

〈**Example**〉

a   What do you usually do when you are very happy? --When I am very happy, I jump and shout.

b   What do you usually do when you are lonely? --When I am lonely, I meet a friend and talk.

c   What do you usually do when you are tired? --When I am tired, I drink a cup of tea.

d   What do you usually do when you are bored? --When I am bored, I go downtown and go window shopping.

e   What do you usually do when you are successful? --When I am successful, I say thank you to God.

f   What do you usually do when you cannot sleep at night? --When I cannot sleep at night, I drink a cup of warm milk.

Communication: Giving Advice

Unit 15 で習った、伝わりやすく自然な英文を書く実習として、悩み相談へのアドバイスを書いてみましょう。以下に紹介するのは、皆さんと同年代の人々が書いた悩み相談の手紙です。その中のどれか一つに、アドバイスを書きましょう。後で、同じ悩みにアドバイスをした人同士で集まって、それぞれのアドバイスをシェアしましょう。

⟨Example 1⟩

Dear Sir/Madam,

Although I am twenty-one years old, I have never gone out with a man. My friends say, "Don't worry," but it is quite a serious problem for me!! All my female friends have gone out with guys, so they often talk about their love stories. Whenever such a conversation starts, naturally I cannot join it. I want a boyfriend, but I do not have anyone I like among my acquaintances. Some have asked me out, but I have always refused. I may have too high an ideal for guys, but I do not want to compromise. What should I do?

Loving Rabbit

⟨Example 2⟩

I belong to a club. When I joined it, I enjoyed the group activities. But now, I am not very happy when I think about the club because I worry about my relationships. I am shy, so I am poor at speaking. I try to speak but I don't succeed. The more I think that I have to say something, the more tensed up I am. And I can't think of what to say.

I want to talk naturally and enjoy the club. What should I do? Please tell me.

Boss

⟨Example 3⟩

A friend of mine has a problem with her part-time job. She works at a bookstore. She receives 950 yen for an hour. That is a very low wage. She thinks that she can get a better job. I think so, too. But it is difficult for her to quit working at the store because her fellow workers are kind to her and she likes them very much. But I hope that she can solve her problem. How can I give advice to her about it?

Silvia

⌐〈**Example 4**〉────────────────────────────────────

Lately, I think I have to study harder, but I often yield to temptations and watch interesting TV programs and net surf. As a result, I just continue watching TV and doing surfing. I stay up late almost every day and go to bed at 3:00 or 4:00.

I have fallen into a bad habit of being lazy. I want to get over my bad habit and study harder, but I can't easily concentrate on studying. What should I do?

James

引用文献

HOOPLAKIDZ RHYMES シーズン 8・エピソード 6　'This is the House that Jack Built Song'.
（https://www.youtube.com/watch?v=7sDSYVfnj_E）

'Jaremaga'.（catchawave.jp/jm/）

The History Place: Great Speeches Collection.　（https://www.historyplace.com/speeches/vest.htm）

《著者紹介》

三浦　孝（みうら・たかし）

大学卒業後23年間高校英語教師を勤め、バーミンガム大学院通信課程に学びM.A.取得。名古屋明徳短大、静岡大学教育学部に奉職の後、2013年に静岡大学を定年退職、同大学名誉教授。現在はバーミンガム大学院通信課程と人間環境大学にて非常勤講師、ヒューマニスティック英語教育研究会会長。著書（共著含む）は『だから英語は教育なんだ』『ヒューマンな英語授業がしたい』『高校英語授業を知的にしたい』『英語授業への人間形成的アプローチ』（いずれも研究社）等。

Discovery Learning in English Structure for Communication
——〈発見型〉コミュニケーション英文法

2020年11月30日　初版発行

著　者●三浦 孝

Copyright © 2020 Miura Takashi

発行者　吉田尚志
発行所　株式会社 研究社
　　　　〒102-8152 東京都千代田区富士見 2-11-3

　　　　電話　営業 03-3288-7777（代）　編集 03-3288-7711（代）
　　　　振替　00150-9-26710
　　　　http://www.kenkyusha.co.jp/

英 文 校 閲●Douglas S. Jarrell
朗　　　　読●Xanthe Smith, Peter Serafin
装丁デザイン●株式会社 明昌堂（相羽裕太）
本 文 組 版●株式会社 明昌堂（梅田理恵）
印刷所●研究社印刷株式会社

KENKYUSHA
〈検印省略〉

ISBN 978-4-327-42201-1　C1082　　　Printed in Japan